SOUTH GERMAN SCULPTURE 1480–1530

VICTORIA AND ALBERT MUSEUM

South German Sculpture 1480–1530

by MICHAEL BAXANDALL

London: Her Majesty's Stationery Office
1974

Museum Monograph No. 26
ISBN 0 11 290163 8

CONTENTS

FOREWORD

For the text of this publication, as for that of the illustrated booklet *German Wood Statuettes 1500–1800*, HMSO, 1967, we are indebted to Mr Michael Baxandall of the Warburg Institute, who was formerly in the Department of Architecture and Sculpture. He wishes to acknowledge much advice and information given him by Professor Theodor Müller and Dr Alfred Schädler of the Bayerisches Nationalmuseum, Munich.

Terence Hodgkinson
Keeper, Department of Architecture and Sculpture

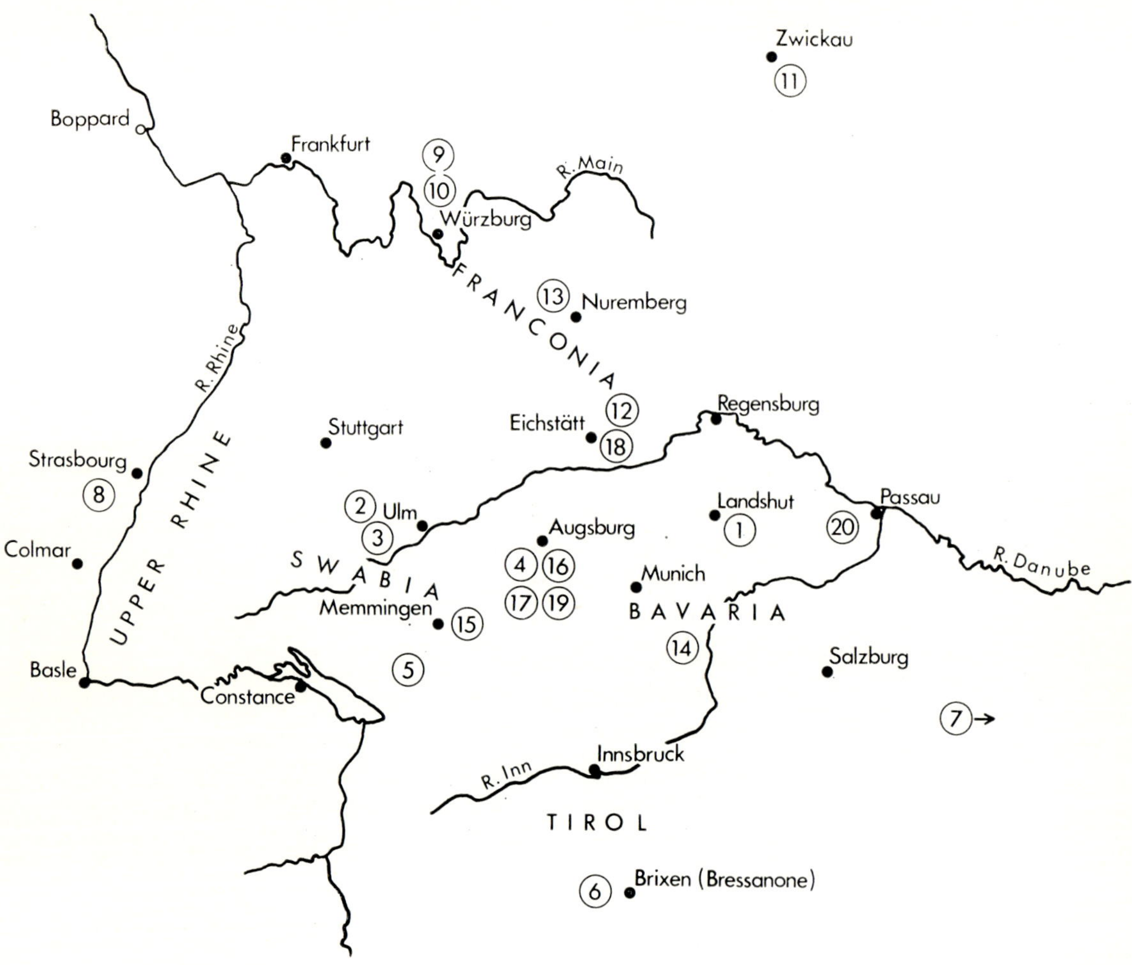

Zwickau
11
Boppard
Frankfurt
9
10
R. Main
Würzburg
FRANCONIA
13
Nuremberg
R. Rhine
12
Regensburg
Stuttgart
Eichstätt
18
Strasbourg
8
UPPER RHINE
2
Ulm
3
Landshut
1
Passau
20
Augsburg
Colmar
SWABIA
4
16
Munich
R. Danube
Memmingen
17
19
BAVARIA
15
14
Basle
5
Salzburg
Constance
7
Innsbruck
R. Inn
TIROL
6
Brixen (Bressanone)

INTRODUCTION

In the years round 1500 – the years between the union of Burgundy and Hapsburg in 1477 and the crystallizing of the Reformation in the Confession of Augsburg in 1530 – there was a sudden creative outburst among the sculptors of south Germany. Along with the Romanesque-Gothic and the Baroque-Rococo periods, it is one of three great episodes in the history of German sculpture. The art of this period is often called 'Late Gothic' and sometimes called 'Early Renaissance', and really belongs to both. If the term 'Transitional' were not already in use for something quite different, it would fit this sculpture very well: as it is, 'Late Gothic' remains the common term for it, with an occasional appeal to 'Early Renaissance' when Italian or antique influences are very clear. A last resort is to refer to the 'Age of Dürer' (1471–1528), or to the 'Dürer period'.

Romanesque-Gothic and Baroque-Rococo sculptures are usually an integral part of great buildings: for this reason no museum can hope to represent them at all adequately in its galleries. But Late Gothic–Early Renaissance sculpture is usually distinct from the building in which it was housed; it is more self-contained, or at least detachable. Therefore it is the best sort of German sculpture one can expect to find either in a museum or outside Germany itself. This publication, which is not an exhaustive catalogue, is intended as a guide to the small but interesting collection of south German sculpture of the period in the Victoria and Albert Museum. North German sculpture, which is poorly represented in the Museum, is not included.

Two kinds of preliminary information can help one to understand these carvings. One kind is about the physical means and circumstances of the art; the other is about the interplay of styles between artist and artist, town and town, town and hinterland.

I

Most of the sculpture made by the Late Gothic carvers was in wood, particularly limewood. The use of limewood is one of the things that distinguishes south German from north German sculptors, who used harder wood, particularly oak, and also from French sculptors, who favoured walnut. Limewood has special qualities. Unlike stone it is light and elastic, lends itself to cutting in thin sheets and into sharp-edged forms, and must not be left in large solid masses, since these crack as the wood ages. Unlike such dense hardwoods as oak, it cuts easily, is not much marked by grain, and can be carved in all directions: it is the nearest a deciduous tree can come to softwood. The physical character of limewood influenced the forms of south German sculpture very much. They are excavated freely and deeply, with great membranes of wood swinging out from the main body, and they avoid the solidity that limewood cannot sustain as it dries: a limewood figure is often hollowed out inside, too, until it becomes a cylinder of sapwood with the heartwood removed. The carvers pressed the limewood character of their style to the limit, sometimes even using green unseasoned wood – as Veit Stoss is known to have done for one of his greatest works – which would cut the more freely but presented extreme difficulties of design if it were not to crack as the wood dried out. The limewood character also impressed itself on their work in other materials. When Tilman Riemenschneider had to design a series of sandstone figures, he carved them in limewood in the limewood style and then let masons struggle to carry out his designs in the stone. So one worthwhile way of looking at a piece of this German sculpture is as a form resolving a special problem: how to carve a block of wood in such a way that, while the volume it inhabits remains large, the matter will be able to shrink without breaking.

The main tools with which the sculptor cut his wood were: the axe and the adze, with which he did much of the roughing out; the drill, which was used for much of the deeper excavation; and various chisels, including chisels with skewed blades (fig. 1). The carvings were meticulously finished with knives and by abrasion, and exploit the contrast between broad smooth areas and sharply cut local detail. It is sometimes helpful, too, in understanding the configuration of folds in a figure's drapery, to remember that a figure was not cut in an upright position, but lying on its back.

For much of the period most sculptures were painted polychrome, after the wood had been prepared with a gesso ground. The drapery was partly gilt with gold leaf and partly painted with resin-bound or tempera-bound colours: white, blue, madder, red lead, green and a few others. Flesh was painted much as in panel-pictures, with pigments and glazes laid over a red base. But by the 1490s some sculptors were producing sculpture without this polychromy. That is not to say that the wood was left raw: new untreated limewood has an undistinguished yellowish colour and is quickly discoloured by dust. Therefore these sculptors finished their monochrome work with transparent glazes, often tinted a brown wood-colour: the glaze

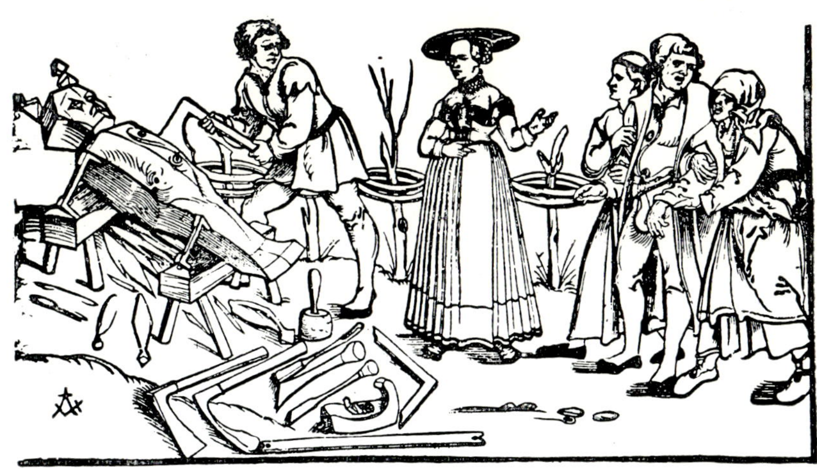

Fig. 1. The sculptor and his tools. Woodcut for a broadsheet by Erhard Schoen (d. 1542).

on an unpigmented altarpiece by Riemenschneider was analysed recently and it consisted of white of egg, oil, lime, white-lead, black and ochre. Between the fully polychrome and the fully monochrome there were intermediate types: many wood-coloured pieces have pigmented eyes and lips, and a few disconcertingly have flesh-coloured faces and wood-coloured drapery. But nearly all the bare wood sculptures one now sees are like that because they have been stripped of their original polychromy (no. 9), or – as still, unfortunately, happens – because the original monochrome glaze has been mistaken for nineteenth century varnish and removed. In general, as the gesso and paint covering of sculpture gave way to the thin glazes, the detail of the carving became finer and the carver's skill more assertive.

The carver's staple product was not the single figure, but complex structures containing a number of figures. Much the most important of these was the winged retable (fig. 2): that is, an altarpiece consisting of a central framed compartment (the *Corpus*) with hinged doors on each side (the *Flügel*). These doors were usually decorated with scenes or figures on both sides, so that the altarpiece had two faces – a simpler one when closed, and a resplendent one when open. Under the *Corpus* there was often a type of predella (the *Sarg*), and above the *Corpus* a crowning superstructure of finials and figures (the *Gesprenge* or *Aufsatz*). This type of retable could be varied in many ways, but the commonest type has a central *Corpus* housing figures in full relief, and wings decorated on the inside with low relief sculpture or paintings and on the outside with paintings. It was the sculpture that was displayed when the retable was open.

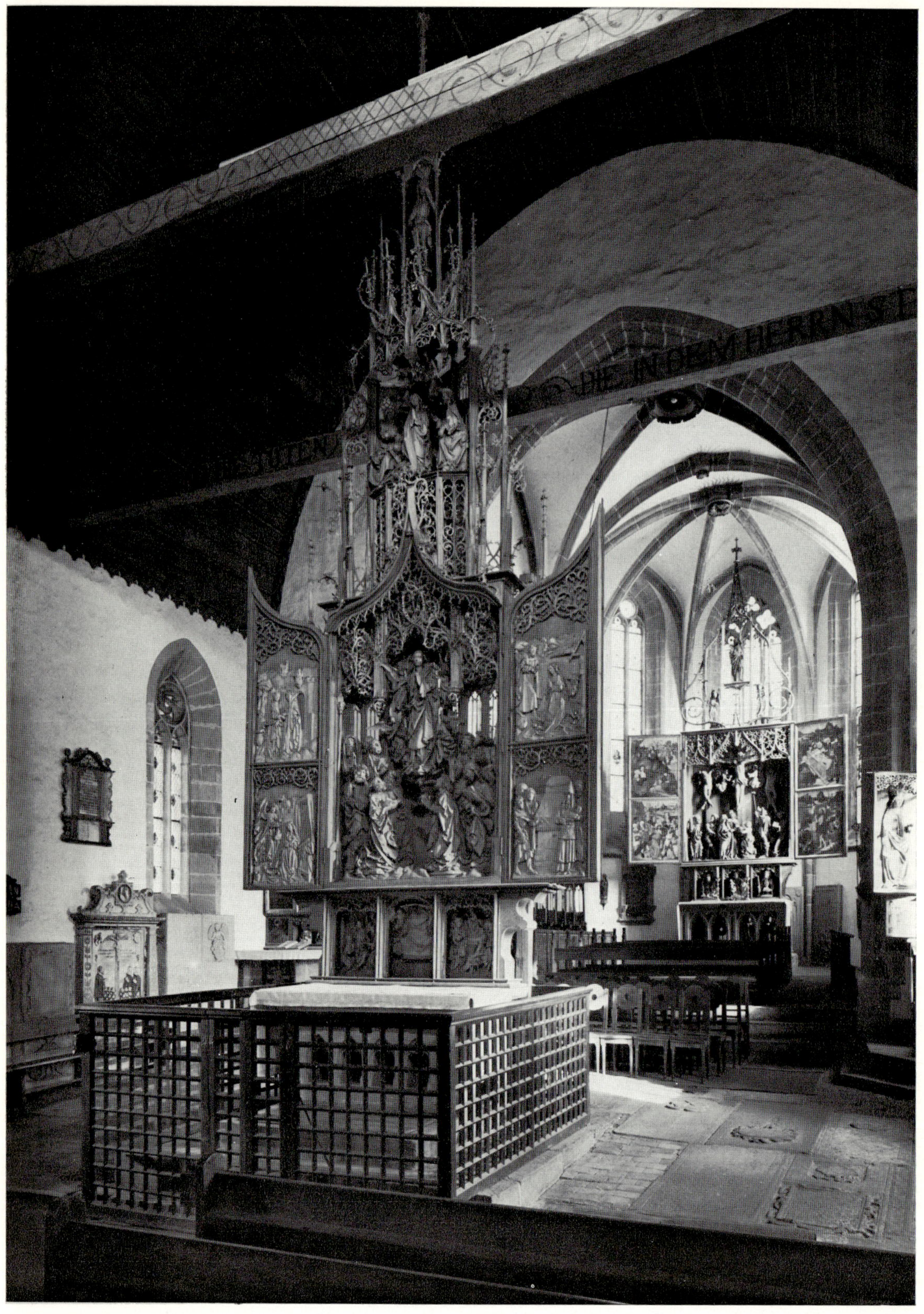
DIE IN DEM HERRN

The size of these retables varied from small domestic altarpieces a foot or so high, to great structures like that made over a period of twelve years by Veit Stoss at Cracow, more than forty feet high. They combined pictures, statues, ornament and miniature architecture and brought together painters, sculptors and joiners in a single enterprise. The contractor and designer might be either a painter or a sculptor, but no one man made all of the retable: he hired journeyman practitioners of other arts to complement his own, or he sub-contracted parts of the work to other workshops. Therefore even a signature on a retable is not always a sure way of knowing who carved a given figure on it. A more positive point about the retables is that they constituted a frame for sculpture, since the complex of foliate shrinework established the artist's own context. At the least it was a buffer between the sculptor's figures and what lay outside, and made him independent of the style of the building in which the sculpture was to stand: in this the late gothic sculptor was freer than either the high gothic or the baroque artist. At its best the shrinework was much more than a buffer. It became a semi-abstract zone of pattern responsive to the representational pattern of drapery and figure movement: each counterpointed the other.

In the fourteenth century most German sculptors had been attached to the workshops of the great churches. In the fifteenth they had increasingly left these centres and established themselves in smaller independent workshops, often in quite small towns. Of course, some sculptors still worked in cathedral workshops (no. 1), but these were not usually the most progressive spirits: the best opportunities now often lay outside. In the towns carvers and other artists were organized into guilds, which played a more important role in Germany than in Italy. The guilds had developed in the earlier fifteenth century during a period of increased competition that was caused by a growth in the number of craftsmen. The vigour and regulations of a guild varied from town to town, and many of the rules have no direct bearing on the style of the art: but the guilds did set out to raise the standards of their craft in certain specific ways. They protected the customer by regulating the quality of wood and of such materials as gold leaf and ultramarine. They regulated the sculptor's career from apprentice to journeyman, and from journeyman to master, so as to limit the number of masters and ensure their competence. Above all they took a keen interest in the size of workshops and the number of assistants working in them. The most common limit set on this was a maximum of two apprentices and a proportionate number of journeymen, but there were some towns which set no effective limit and

Fig. 2.
Carved altarpiece of the Life of the Virgin in the Herrgottskirche, Creglingen, South Germany. By Tilman Riemenschneider (c. 1460–1531). Photograph by Helga Schmidt-Glassner.

had very large workshops indeed. The distinction between large workshop carvings and small workshop carvings is a basic distinction of style. Tilman Riemenschneider of Würzburg (nos. 9–10), maintaining a very large workshop in a town without effective limits, developed a subtly economic style adapted to delegation and rapid production. Veit Stoss of Nuremberg (no. 13), who did not have a large workshop, made figures in which a much higher proportion of the carving is conspicuously master's work, virtuoso cutting designed to be recognized as such.

A large undertaking like a retable altarpiece was subject to a formal contract between the artist and the client. The contract would supplement verbal specifications about the quality of materials and the general layout with a detailed drawing (*Visierung*) of the work, to which the patron had agreed and the craftsman must conform. On the other hand, it seems that many sculptors kept a stock of smaller sculpture of standard type, Madonnas and Crucifixes and so on, and some sculptors, including Veit Stoss himself, took their wares to the great fairs held in such towns as Frankfurt. The difference between the Museum's two Riemenschneider works (nos. 9–10) is also probably the difference between bespoke and ready-made carving. In either case, the client was himself likely to be a mercantile man not very unlike the master sculptor himself. The sculpture was paid for less often by religious foundations or territorial princes than by the commercial men of the towns – or by confraternities of such men – and in this sense Late Gothic sculpture is a bourgeois art. How much one will want to make of this fact is a matter of taste.

II

South Germany was a region of relatively small towns. The five largest – Strasbourg, Ulm, Augsburg, Nuremberg and Regensburg – had between 20,000 and 40,000 people living in them; this was not much, compared with the 200,000 of Paris or 100,000 of Florence, or even with the 50,000 of Ghent or Bruges. On the whole, only the largest south German towns were able consistently to maintain more than a few substantial sculpture workshops at a time, and in practice the five are reduced to three. Ulm and Augsburg worked rather as one centre, with the initiative gradually passing from Ulm to Augsburg; and for various reasons Regensburg, a city with a splendid High Gothic tradition, never quite played the part in Late Gothic that one might have expected. So there were three primary centres with a metropolitan role: Strasbourg serving the Upper Rhine; Ulm-Augsburg dominating Swabia and exporting much work southwards into eastern Switzerland and the Tirol; and Nuremberg at the centre of Franconia. Smaller towns – Memmingen in Swabia, Eichstätt in Franconia, Zwickau in Saxony and very many others – maintained sculptors who served their immediate area and they occasionally threw up an artist who gained a more than local importance: Tilman Riemenschneider in Würzburg and Hans Leinberger in Landshut are examples of this. Within this general scheme there was much movement and cross-fertilization – journeymen wandering from centre to centre to gain experience and learn new models; masters travelling to a commission, or works of sculpture themselves moving along the roads or rivers from workshop to client; and, more and more, engravings and woodcuts spreading patterns and styles which a sculptor could adapt to his own purposes.

The immediate sources of the Late Gothic–Early Renaissance phase lie in the 1460s and it is convenient to link them particularly with two events – the arrival in Strasbourg of Nikolaus Gerhaerts of Leyden in 1463, and the death of Hans Multscher of Ulm in 1467. Gerhaerts and Multscher are the two pre-eminent stylistic facts at this moment, Gerhaerts a new and disruptive fact, Multscher and his heirs a conservative fact of the local tradition.

Hans Multscher had maintained a large workshop in Ulm that produced both sculpture and painting, and it says much about the extensiveness of his trade that his greatest work should have been the retable of 1456–58 for the church at Sterzing (now Vipiteno) in the Tirol, on the Brenner route to Italy. Multscher's sculpture style was a refined and muscular variant on the tired 'Soft Style', as it is called, into which most German sculpture had lapsed by the middle of the century. He refined and revitalized its mechanical *contrapposto*, and gave freshly sensitive and relevant expressions to his heads and faces. He broke up the stock formulas of looped grooves that had become a substitute for modelled drapery, and related the patterns of his folds to the limbs and movement of the figure and to a complex general composition. He was, in fact, the south German tradition at its best. The number of his own works is limited, but his pupils and imitators are innumerable, and his style was adaptable enough to survive inheritance: Ulm sculpture and most other Swabian sculpture is more or less Multscher-esque until the end of the century (nos. 2–5).

Nikolaus Gerhaerts is a mystery. It is certain he was a Dutchman, but nothing is known about his artistic antecedents or development. He exists in art history as a documented itinerary, a handful of superb sandstone sculptures, and an explosive effect on the south German wood sculptors. The itinerary is short: Trier 1462, Strasbourg and Constance 1463–67, Vienna and Wiener Neustadt 1469–73. That is to say, he moved in a swift arc along first the western and then the southern periphery of south Germany. What little of his work survives is in stone: a great wooden retable he made for the cathedral at Constance was destroyed by iconoclasts during the Reformation, but it was this retable that must have offered the most accessible lesson to the German carvers. It is clear from the stone carvings, and from wood carvings by sculptors under his immediate influence, what the kernel of the lesson must have been. It was that the carver's figure need not be simply the rhythmically grooved and flexed cylinder of the 'Soft Style'; instead, the sculptor could insist on the fact of space lying between the separate limbs of his figure, and he could also throw out bursts of drapery far from the figure itself. It seems to have been an intoxicating release for the German carvers, so much so that one gets an impression of Gerhaerts having triggered off rather than created a reaction. At any rate, wherever Gerhaerts had worked, limewood sculptors started cutting deep and free, and in the 1470s and 1480s these sculptors moved into south Germany from the periphery.

So it is sometimes a helpful over-simplification to see the later fifteenth century sculpture in terms of an interaction between two basic styles, represented by Multscher and Gerhaerts. At the centre, in the great sculpture-producing city of Ulm, is the refined and restrained Multscher style, conservative in the best sense, re-formulating the best elements in the native tradition into a mature and coherent method, itself open to further development; Swabia is the homeland of this style. From the southern and western periphery – from Strasbourg, Constance, Passau, Vienna – move the sculptors and patterns of the Gerhaerts style, flourishing their drapery and keying up their figures. And to the north and the east, in Franconia and Bavaria, strong local traditions like that of Nuremberg and Regensburg-Landshut, often deriving from the workshops of great churches, interacted with both these styles to produce new variants of their own.

In outline this was the stage on which the many hundreds of south German sculptors worked in the last quarter of the fifteenth century and the first years of the sixteenth. The individual sculptor's style is usually defined in terms of a conditioning by a regional training ('Nuremberg' say, or 'South Swabian'), then in terms of a degree of dependence on one or other of a few great inventive personalities in the art. It is these few great artists who give the Late Gothic sculpture its special quality, and through whom it is best approached. An uncontroversial list of them would be headed by Michael Pacher of Bruneck, Veit Stoss of Nuremberg (no. 13), Tilman Riemenschneider of Würzburg (nos. 9-10), and Michel and Gregor Erhart of Ulm and Augsburg (no. 4), closely followed by a dozen others little less original.

Michael Pacher was the great master of the southern periphery. His headquarters were in Bruneck (Brunico) in the Tirol and from here he made sorties, ranging from Bozen (Bolzano) to Salzburg, to furnish retable altarpieces combining both painting and sculpture. Pacher painting was much influenced by Venice and Padua, but Pacher sculpture owes nothing to Italy. It is developed out of Multscher – who had worked for the Tirol – and the Upper Rhenish followers of Gerhaerts. The best of his surviving works is the altar in the pilgrimage church of St Wolfgang in the Salzkammergut (1471–81), an astonishingly rich and subtly ordered complex of figures and shrinework, so heavily gilt that it is practically monochrome. Pacher died in 1498 while he was finishing at Salzburg what was the biggest of all the Late Gothic retables. His influence on the very productive Tirolese workshops of Bruneck (Brunico) and Brixen (Bressanone) (no. 6) was a lasting one.

Veit Stoss was a Nuremberg-trained Swabian. From 1477 until 1496 he was in Cracow in Poland, making his large altarpiece for the church of the German community and also a red marble tomb for King Casimir IV. The altarpiece, unlike Pacher's, had no paintings but consisted of brightly polychromed sculpture; its figures gesticulate violently in angular poses contrasting with the curvilinear sweep and swirl of their drapery. After his return to Nuremberg in 1496 Stoss's career had its ups and downs. He quickly became the leading wood sculptor there – as Adam Kraft was the stone sculptor and Peter Vischer the bronze sculptor – but he was always a small-workshop artist. It seems that he was identified with a highly personal woodcarving style, well represented by the London statuette (no. 13), in which the whipping curves of the full outer drapery are the main basis for the design. A Stoss figure is a sort of three-dimensional line drawing. It may be that in the many superb carvings in this vein he was partly the prisoner of his own established style, a trade-mark he was trapped by: the London figure certainly seems to offer itself as a 'typical' Stoss. What is also certain is that when, towards the end of his career, his own son was in a position to commission from him an altarpiece, now at Bamberg

(1520–23), he switched suddenly to a less spectacular style. His influence was felt not only in Franconia, but also in Poland.

Tilman Riemenschneider's position in Würzburg, of which he became Burgomaster, was dominant enough for him to override any guild restriction there may have been and to maintain a large workshop: between 1501 and 1517 he registered twelve apprentices, and the nineteen known retables from his shop were only a part of his work. Production on this scale demands a measure of standardization and the details of his work – the eyes, hands, beards and so on – are from a range of economical, simply carved, easily delegated formulas repeated again and again in continually new combinations (no. 9). But the fluent simplicity of Riemenschneider's shop had its own virtues. Like no other sculptor's, the forms of his work are the forms natural to limewood, because they are designed to be easy in it. Where Stoss was masterful and aggressive in his relation to the wood, doing what was conspicuously difficult, Riemenschneider took a more feminine role. A good piece of his sculpture is half representation, half conversation with a material (no. 10). Riemenschneider has suffered very much from modern sentimentalization; the beautiful reverse curves of a Riemenschneider hand or cheek-bone, the asymmetry of any pair of Riemenschneider eyes, have been seen as expressive of extreme sensibility, when they are really eloquent of the supremely free and fluent run of a blade through soft sapwood. Because so many apprentices and journeymen spent time in his workshop his influence went far (no. 11).

Michel and Gregor Erhart of Ulm were father and son, and it is often difficult to draw a line between them. In an altar at Blaubeuren near Ulm (1493–94) that has its original polychromy still in perfect condition, they brought the progressive Ulm style to its climax. Multscher is still very much present in this sculpture, but enriched and enlivened by much else. The Erharts were the masters of a gentle, tentative *contrapposto*, only half veiled by the complex patterns of their drapery, since flesh and cloth seem somehow fused into one consistency. In 1494 Gregor moved to Augsburg and took citizenship: much of his work there was fine, small-scale sculpture (no. 4) and his influence was decisive for such young Augsburg sculptors as Hans Daucher (no. 16). Gregor Erhart, more than anyone else, links the art of Multscher and Gerhaerts with new styles developed in the next century.

For Stoss (d. 1533), Riemenschneider (d. 1531) and Erhart (d. 1540) take one quite deep into the sixteenth century, since they were all still active in the 1520s; yet some time before this the nature of the sculpture trade and the demands on the sculptor had changed. Between 1510 and 1520 the great boom in polychrome retables had passed its peak. There were many reasons for this: the rhythm of fashion, new Italianate standards of artistic restraint, a loss in social self-confidence by patrician and burgess patrons, the first stirrings of the Reformation, and others. In any event, the results were plain and added up to a crisis for the sculptors which became progressively more acute in the 1520s as the uncertainties and the sometimes straight anti-figurative temper of the early Reformation inhibited patrons still further (no. 16).

Two main kinds of work belong to this last stage. In the first place, retable sculptures were still being made, particularly in securely Catholic areas, and with the younger sculptors these tended to an exacerbated Late Gothic that is sometimes, misleadingly but forgivably, called its 'baroque' phase (no. 14). The two masterpieces of this style are the great Hans Leinberger's altar at Moosburg near Landshut in Bavaria (1511–14) and the Master H. L.'s altar in the church at Breisach near Colmar on the Upper Rhine (1526). They differ from each other in many ways, but what they have in common is that both know something of Italian art, and both have reacted against aspects of it: there is an element of German backlash in an Italianizing period. Neither Leinberger nor H. L. is represented in London – neither is adequately represented in any museum – and in general this phase is properly seen only in German churches.

The other current is well represented in London. When the demand for retables began to fall off, the sculptors were forced to develop new genres, smaller in scale and less public. Any sculptor working in these years was affected: the Museum possesses Veit Stoss's response to the situation (no. 13). But a new generation of sculptors turned particularly to relief sculpture, and a leader among these was Gregor Erhart's nephew Hans Daucher. In his earlier years he worked with his father on at least two large-scale complexes of stone sculpture, but even by 1518 he had also evolved a type of small relief in fine limestone quarried at Solnhofen, between Augsburg and Nuremberg: it is the same stone and from the same quarry as that on which Aloys Senefelder invented lithography in 1798. Many other sculptors followed Hans Daucher's example (no. 19), and a typical carving of the 1520s is a small virtuoso relief (nos. 18–20), in Solnhofen stone or in pear or boxwood. It is likely to have taken ideas and sometimes a complete composition from engravings or woodcuts (figs. 3–5); but much of its interest will lie in the tension of a large-scale monumental style adapting itself to a small format, and as the adaptation becomes more complete over the years the interest becomes less. The 1530s –

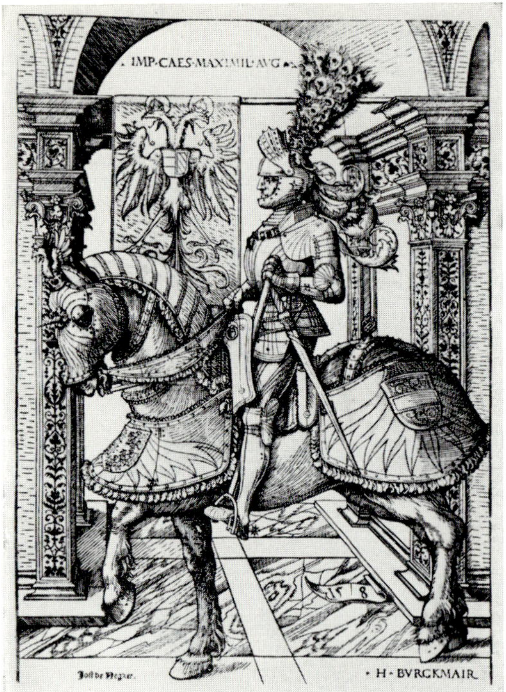

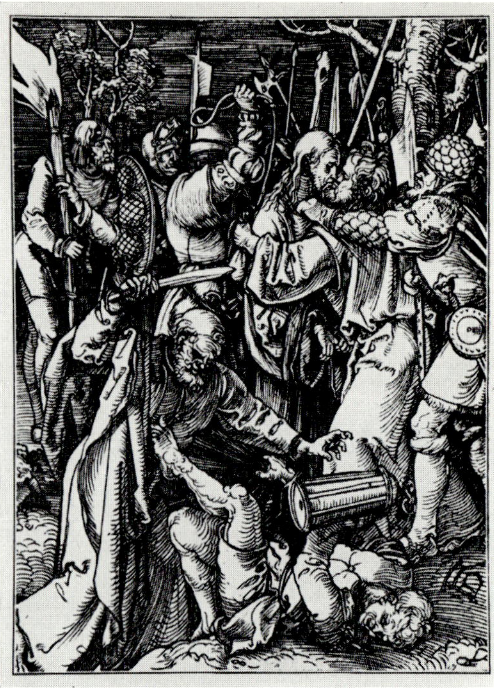

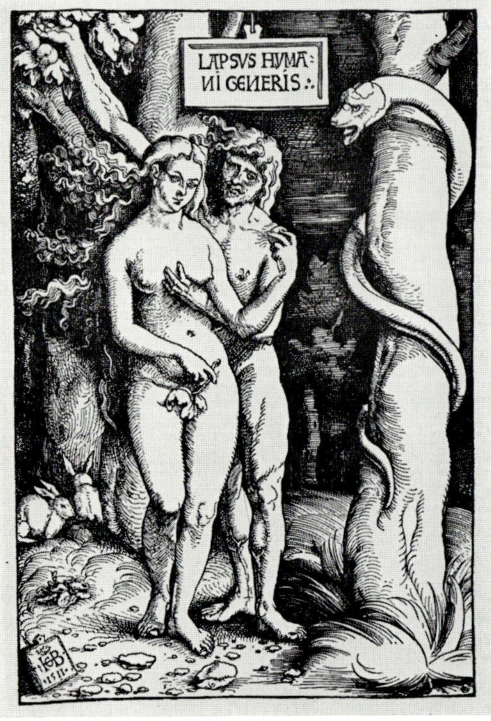

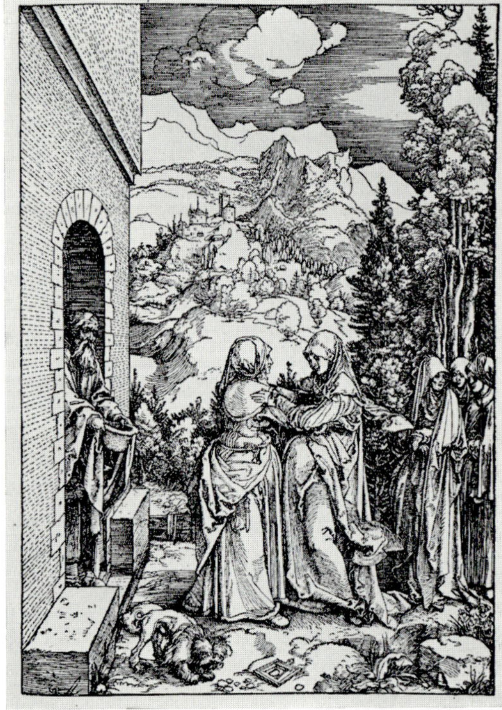

Fig. 3. *The Emperor Maximilian I.* Woodcut. By Hans Burgkmair (1473–1531). See no. 19.

Fig. 4. *The Taking of Christ.* Woodcut. By Albrecht Dürer (1471–1528). See no. 17.

Fig. 5. *The Fall.* Woodcut. By Hans Baldung Grien (1484 or 1485–1545). See no. 18.

Fig. 6. *The Visitation.* Woodcut. By Albrecht Dürer (1471–1528). See no. 8.

blander, less pressed by memories of the limewood retable style, more and more skilfully Italianate – are no longer part of German Late Gothic.

In the late 1530s the Nuremberg engraver and sculptor Peter Flötner published some prints of soldiers, and underneath the prints were doggerel verses telling how these men were craftsmen fallen on hard times. One of them was a sculptor:

Veyt Pildhawer
Vil schöner Pild hab ich geschnitten
Künstlich auf welsch und deutschen sitten
Wiewol die Kunst yetz nimmer gilt . . .

Veit the sculptor.
Many fine figures have I carved with skill,
In German or Italian styles, at will;
Though skill now counts for nothing . . .

It is lack of work that has driven him to be a halberdier. The verses on Veit's predicament point to the two external things that killed Late Gothic sculpture: the diversion of public interest from the sculptor's products and an invasion by new foreign fashions; the Reformation and the Italian style. German sculpture did not have a strong character of its own again till the seventeenth century and the birth of a native baroque.

SHORT BIBLIOGRAPHY

E. F. Bange, *Die Kleinplastik der deutschen Renaissance*, Florence/Munich, 1928.

J. Bier, *Tilman Riemenschneider*, vol. i, Würzburg, 1925; vol. ii, Augsburg, 1930.

S. Dettloff, *Wit Stosz*, Wrocław, 1961.

A. Feulner and T. Müller, *Geschichte der deutschen Plastik*, Munich, 1953.

E. Hessig, *Die Kunst des Meisters E. S. und die Plastik der Spätgotik*, Berlin, 1935.

H. Huth, *Künstler und Werkstatt der Spätgotik*, Augsburg, 1925.

Karlsruhe, Badisches Landesmuseum, *Spätgotik am Oberrhein*, exhibition catalogue, Karlsruhe, 1970.

G. Lill, *Hans Leinberger*, Munich, 1942.

E. Lutze, *Veit Stoss*, Berlin, 1940.

T. Müller, *Alte bairische Bildhauer*, Munich, 1950.

T. Müller, *Bayerisches Nationalmuseum, München, Die Bildwerke in Holz, Ton und Stein, 1450–1540*, Munich, 1959.

T. Müller, *Sculpture in the Netherlands, Germany, France and Spain, 1400–1500*, Pelican History of Art, Harmondsworth, 1966.

G. von der Osten and H. Vey, *Painting and sculpture in Germany and the Netherlands 1500–1600*, Pelican History of Art, Harmondsworth, 1969.

G. Otto, *Die Ulmer Plastik der Spätgotik*, Reutlingen, 1927.

G. Otto, *Gregor Erhart*, Berlin, 1943.

W. Paatz, *Süddeutsche Schnitzaltäre der Spätgotik*, Heidelberg, 1963.

W. Pinder, *Die deutsche Plastik vom ausgehenden Mittelalter bis zum Ende der Renaissance*, vol. ii, Berlin, 1924.

N. Rasmo, *Michael Pacher*, Munich, 1969.

A. Schädler, *Deutsche Plastik der Spätgotik*, Königstein, 1962.

M. Tripps, *Hans Multscher*, Weissenhorn, 1969.

H. Wilm, *Die gotische Holzfigur*, 3rd ed., Stuttgart, 1962.

No. 1 ST PETER AND ST PAUL

Bavarian (Landshut). About 1480

Terracotta, painted. H. 3 ft 4½ in. (102·9 cm.), each figure.
Museum nos. A.37 & A.38-1910

Both figures are chipped on the surface. Fingers of the left hand of A.38-1910 are broken, and St Paul's usual attribute, a sword, is probably also missing. Both figures are hollowed out at the back. The paint – blue robe and red cloak for St Peter, blue robe and green cloak for St Paul – is not original, but may reflect the original hues. Both figures have traces of a gilt border on the cloaks. Overpainting was removed in 1959.

Bought in Innsbruck, 1910 (Gebrüder Colli).

The figures are designed to be set quite high up, probably in shallow tabernacles on the piers or pilasters of a church: their downward glance is due to this. They are persuasively associated by Anton Ress with a series of pigmented terracotta figures, half as big again, in the aisles and choir of the Martinskirche in Landshut; and particularly with a sub-group of these including figures of SS Peter and Paul. The head types and drapery patterns are closely related, but the London figures are squatter in their proportions, and less deeply and coherently modelled; this may be due to a difference in size and perhaps in intended position, and they are certainly by a sculptor with experience in the Martinskirche workshops. The Landshut figures belong in the period 1460–80 and the London ones may be put at the end of, or slightly after, the 1470s. A terracotta figure of the Virgin in the Silten collection in Berlin (H. Wilm, *Gotische Tonplastik in Deutschland*, Augsburg, 1929, p. 69 & fig. 119) is in a very similar style.

A. Ress, 'Studien zur Plastik der Martinskirche in Landshut, II, Die Tonplastiken' in *Verhandlungen des Historischen Vereins für Niederbayern*, vol. lxxxi, 1955, pp. 76–81, fig. 11.

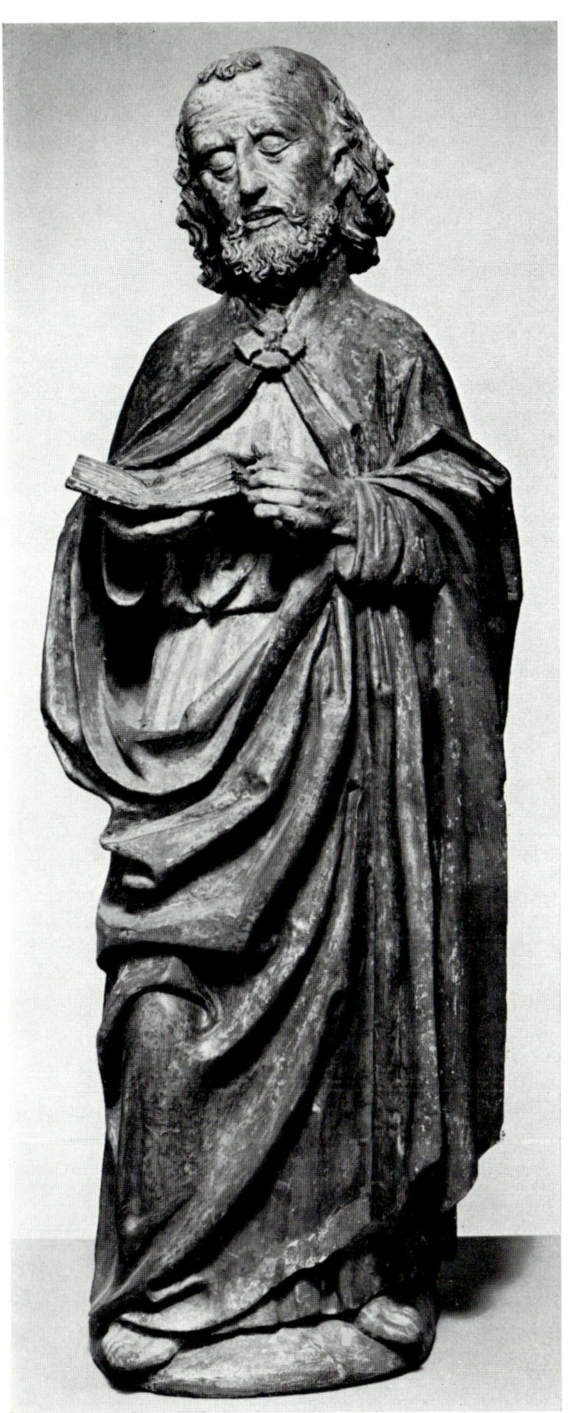
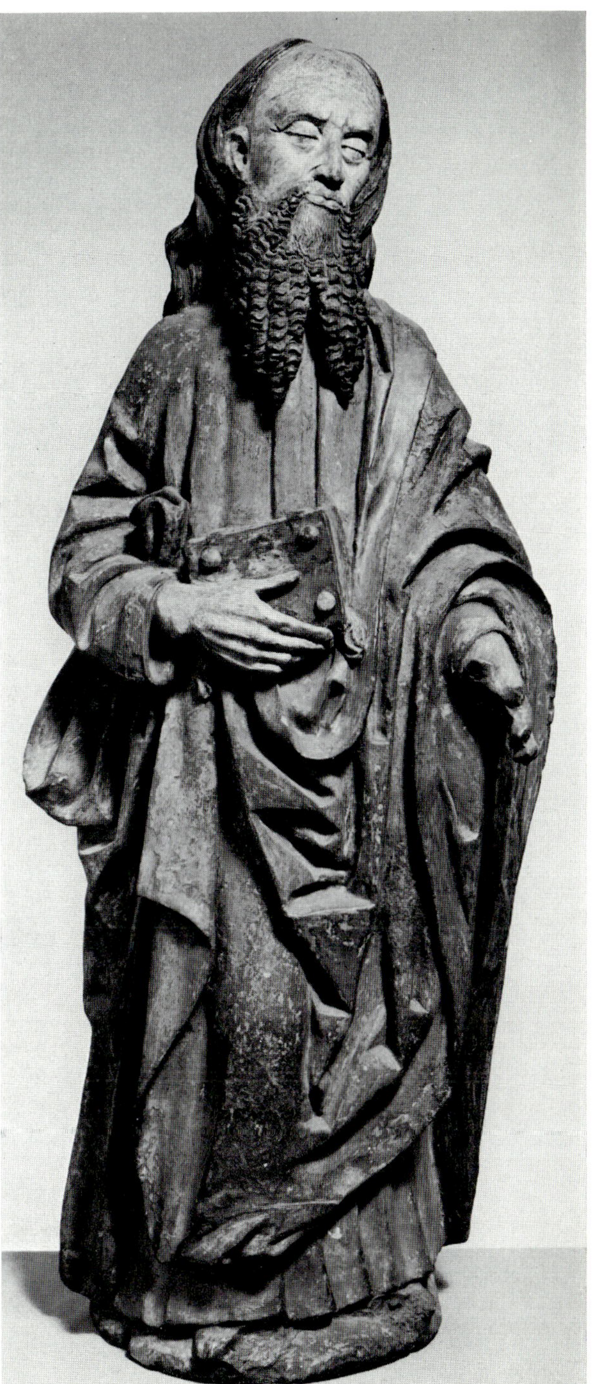

No. 2 A BISHOP

Swabian (Ulm?). About 1480

Limewood, with traces of paint. H. 4 ft (121·9 cm.).
Museum no. 111-1908

The base of the figure is split and chipped. There are extensive traces of green paint, not original, on the alb, cope and dalmatic; of red, green and gold on a rosette on the book cover held by the right hand.

Bought in Frankfurt, 1908.

This is a flanking figure from a group, probably in a small retable altar. Its pose demands a principal figure to its right, to which it inclines its head. The head type and drapery patterns derive from the sculpture of Hans Multscher of Ulm, and the figure is representative of a very large class of sculptures produced in and around Ulm by craftsmen under his influence: for the general drapery type from which the figure derives, see the Virgin and Child in the Klosterkirche at Heggbach (J. Baum, *Die Ulmer Plastik um 1500*, Stuttgart, 1911, pl. 3); for an analogous simplification of Multscher's style, see the Virgin and Child in the Staatliche Sammlungen (Inv. 8145) at Berlin-Dahlem; for the bishop type and for the kind of shrine from which the carving comes, see the figures of St Ulrich and St Conrad in the altar of 1488 from Hausen near Neu-Ulm, removed to Stuttgart (J. Baum, *Kunstsammlungen des Württembergischen Staates*, vol. ii, *Deutsche Bildwerke des Mittelalters*, 1923, pl. 90).

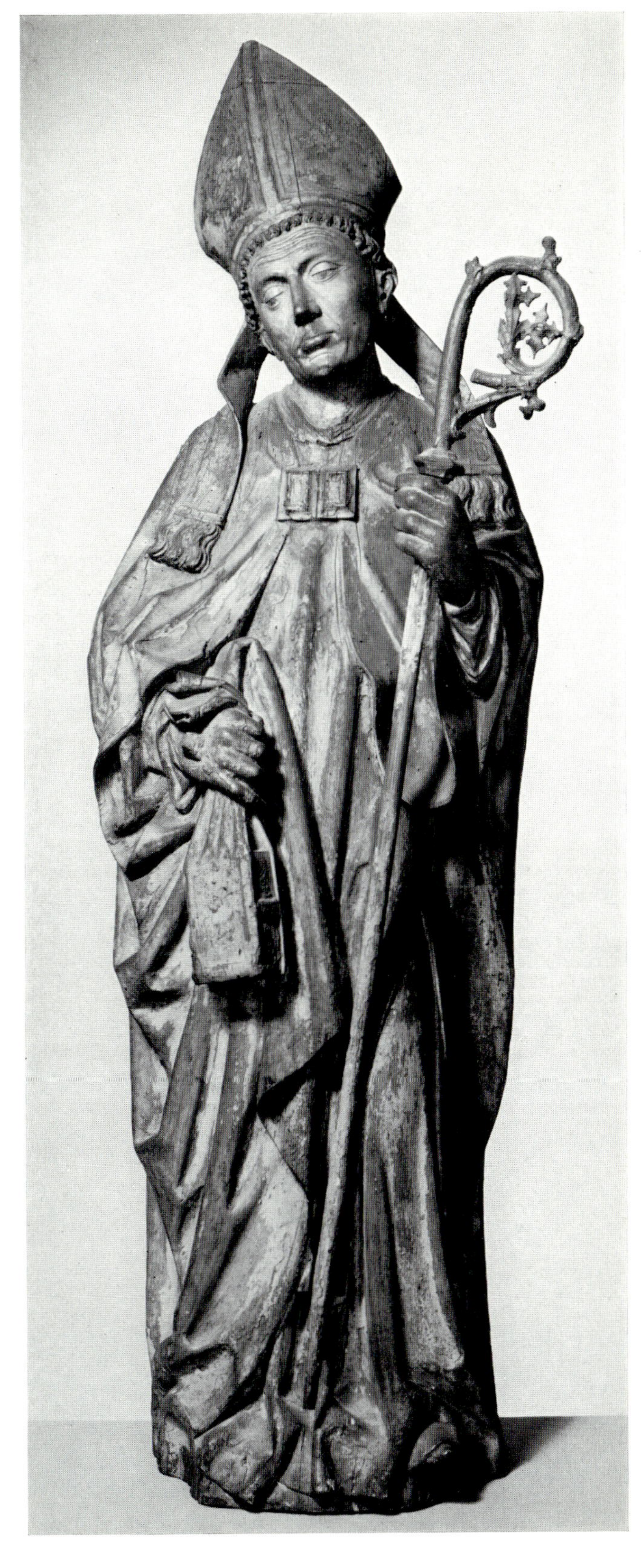

No. 3 THE ADORATION OF THE MAGI

Swabian (Ulm). About 1500–10

Limewood, painted. H. 4 ft 2 in. (126·9 cm.); w. 3 ft 11 in. (119·4 cm.). Museum no. 2418–1856

On each side of the frame are hinges suitable for supporting wings. There are a number of breakages, including the Child's left hand, the fingers of His right hand, and the foliate tracery in the top corners. The polychromy, which is in bad condition, is heavily restored.

Provenance unknown.

The carving is the central section of a small retable. It was attributed in 1911 by Julius Baum to the workshop of the master of the great altar at Blaubeuren, south of Ulm – now identified as Michel and/or Gregor Erhart (see no. 4) of Ulm – dated by him around 1500–10. The relation to the Blaubeuren carvings (which are best illustrated in G. Otto, *Gregor Erhart*, Berlin, 1943, *passim*) is clear. The head types of the Magi all have parallels there, in the St Peter and St John the Baptist and the black Magus respectively. Similarly, the broken arc of the Virgin's hem in the foreground picks up a motif in the Blaubeuren relief of the Nativity. But the London group is relatively coarse and indecisive; the lack of articulation, particularly in the drapery, makes an Erhart design and therefore an origin in the Erhart workshop most unlikely. The carving is by an early sixteenth century Ulm sculptor working under the Erharts' influence.

J. Baum, *Die Ulmer Plastik um 1500*, Stuttgart, 1911, pp. xvi, 168.

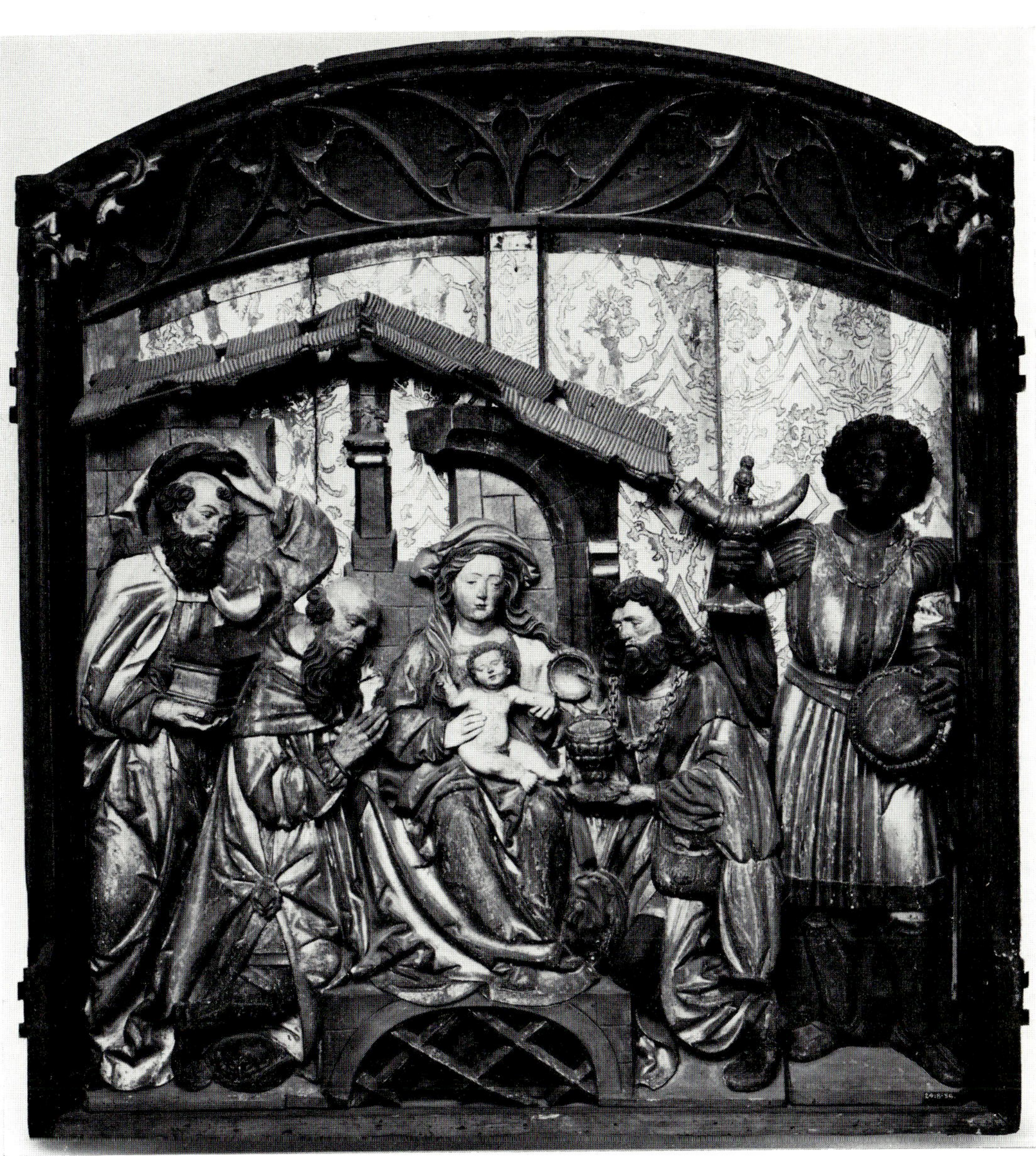

GREGOR ERHART c. 1465–1540

Born around 1465 in Ulm, son of the sculptor Michel Erhart. In 1493–94 he was engaged with his father on the great altarpiece in the Benedictine monastery of Blaubeuren. In 1494 he became a citizen of Augsburg and worked from there for the rest of his career. Hans Daucher (see no. 16) was his nephew. He made over his workshop to his stepson Paulus in 1531 and died at Augsburg in 1540.

No. 4 A YOUNG SAINT AND A VIRGIN SAINT

Gregor Erhart c. 1465–1540
Swabian (Augsburg). About 1500–20

Limewood, with traces of paint. H. $5\frac{5}{16}$ in. (13·5 cm.), and h. $5\frac{5}{8}$ in. (14·3 cm.) respectively.
Museum nos. 6994 & 6995-1860

The present bust-form is not original; the bottom section is roughly cut and stained. On the base of 6994-1860 'Opus Alberti Dureri' has been written with ink in an eighteenth or nineteenth century hand. Several locks of hair have been broken off or chipped on 6994-1860. On both pieces there are clear traces of the outline of pigmented drapery: on 6994-1860 running from the back of the neck over the shoulders, leaving the chest bare; on 6995-1860 running lower across the back, over the shoulders and along the line of the section on the breast. There are minor traces of colour on the eyes and in the mouths.

The heads are listed as 'Adam' and 'Eve', in Josef Scheiger, *Das von Ritter von Schönfeld gegrundete technologische Museum in Wien*, Vienna, 1824 (see E. Leisching, 'Ein Wiener Museum zur Zeit des Wiener Kongresses' in *Kunst und Kunsthandwerk*, vol. xxiv, 1921, p. 97). This collection was assembled by Johann Ferdinand Ritter von Schönfeld between the 1780s and his death in 1821; a proportion was acquired by Schönfeld at the public auction of the Kunst und Schatzkammer of Maximilian II and Rudolf II in Prague in 1782. In 1823 the collection was sold by Schönfeld's son to the Viennese merchant Josef von Dietrich and thence in 1855–56 after depletions to Löwenstein Brothers of Frankfurt, who put it up at Christie's in 1860 under the description of 'the celebrated collection of works of art and vertu known as *The Vienna Museum*'. The heads were bought by the Museum at this sale (12th to 22nd March, nos. 1161–62, as 'by Albert Durer').

The high quality of the heads, the use of limewood rather than a finer-grained material, and the partial pigmentation, suggest that they were carved as models (a) as a basis for negotiations with a client, or (b) for use in the workshop as head types, or (c) for portable silver reliquary

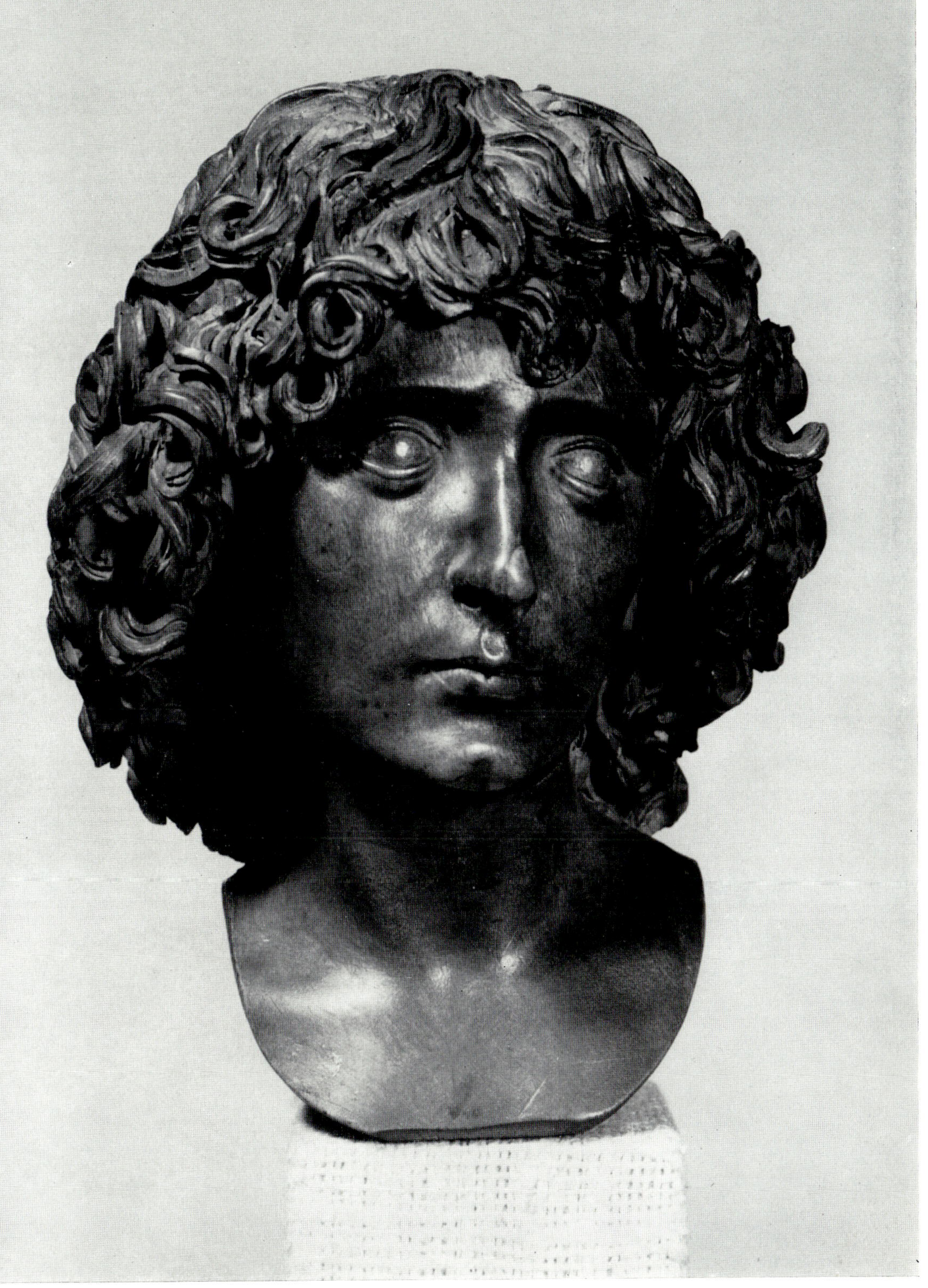

busts or other goldsmith's work (for comparable cases, see: F. Kieslinger, 'Ein spätgotisches Goldschmiedemodell' in *Pantheon*, vol. vi, 1930, pp. 389–90; J. Bier, 'Riemenschneider as a goldsmith's model maker' in *Art Bulletin*, vol. xxxvii, 1955, pp. 103–12). The last possibility is the most likely. The heads have been attributed (1) to Riemenschneider by Bode, Streit, Weber and Tönnies, (2) to a Tirolese sculptor of about 1500 by Schlosser, who ascribed to the same hand a *Vanitas* group in the Kunsthistorisches Museum at Vienna, (3) to Conrat Meit by Winkler and Schrade, (4) to an Upper Rhenish master under Franconian influence by Troescher, (5) to Michel Erhart by Gertrud Otto, and (6) to Gregor Erhart by Müller, Schädler and von der Osten. There is no proper stylistic basis for ascribing the heads to Riemenschneider, Conrat Meit, Tirolese or Upper Rhenish Masters. The types and style of cutting are firmly in the tradition of the Ulm sculptors Michel and Gregor Erhart. In particular, the bust of St John the Evangelist in the predella of the altar at Blaubeuren (1493–94) and the head of the Angel with the Cross from the same altar (G. Otto, *Gregor Erhart*, Berlin, 1943, figs. 31, 50a) represent types which the present heads develop and refine. In handling and, within the limits of the subject, in type there is sufficient similarity between 6994-1860 and the heads of Cistercian monks under the cloak of the Kaisheim *Schutzmantelmadonna* in Berlin (Otto, *op. cit.*, figs. 58, 60), commissioned from Gregor in 1502, to allow attribution to Gregor rather than his father Michel, and to a date not earlier than 1500.

W. Bode, *Geschichte der deutschen Plastik*, Berlin, 1885, p. 166; C. Streit, *Tylman Riemenschneider*, Berlin, 1888, p. 18; A. Weber, *Til Riemenschneider*, Würzburg, 2nd ed., 1888, p. 67, and 3rd ed., 1911, pp. 192, 271; E. Tönnies, *Tilman Riemenschneider*, 1900, pp. 271–72; Burlington Fine Arts Club, *Exhibition of Early German art, Catalogue*, 1906, pp. 118–19; J. von Schlosser, *Werke der Kleinplastik in der Skulpturensammlung des Allerhöchsten Kaiserhauses*, vol. ii, Vienna, 1910, pp. 5–6; F. Winkler, 'Konrad Meits Tätigkeit in Deutschland' in *Jahrbuch der preussischen Kunstsammlungen*, vol. xlv, 1924, p. 45; H. Schrade, *Tilman Riemenschneider*, vol. ii, Heidelberg, 1927, p. 62; G. Troescher, *Conrat Meit von Worms*, Freiburg im Breisgau, 1927, p. 62; G. Otto, *Die Ulmer Plastik der Spätgotik*, Reutlingen, 1927, p. 111, and 'Der Bildhauer Michel Erhart' in *Jahrbuch der preussischen Kunstsammlungen*, vol. lxiv, 1943, pp. 43–4; H. Keller, 'Büste' in *Reallexikon zur deutschen Kunstgeschichte*, vol. iii, 1954, p. 268; T. Müller, *Deutsche Plastik der Renaissance*, Königstein im Taunus, 1963, p. 11; A Schädler in Augsburg, Städtische Kunstsammlungen, *Hans Holbein der Ältere und die Kunst der Spätgotik*, 1965, pp. 186–87; T. Müller, *Sculpture in the Netherlands, Germany, France and Spain*, 1400–1500, Harmondsworth, 1966, p. 174; G. von der Osten and H. Vey, *Painting and sculpture in Germany and the Netherlands, 1500–1600*, Harmondsworth, 1969, p. 34.

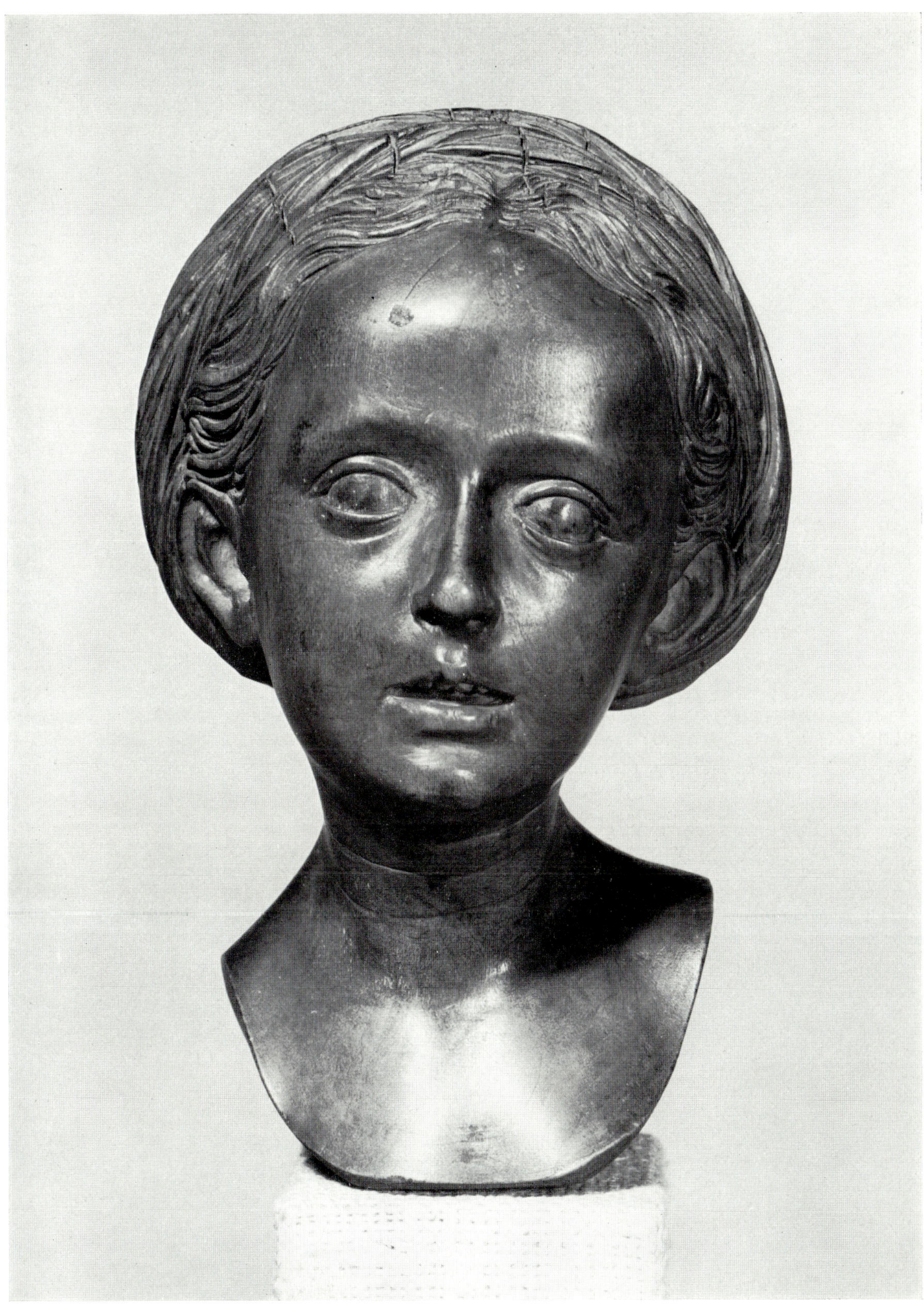

No. 5 CHRIST RIDING ON AN ASS

Swabian. About 1510–20

Limewood, painted. H. 4 ft 10 in. (147·2 cm.).
Museum no. A.1030-1910

The figure is made in two main sections: the upper part of Christ's body in one piece, the lower part and the ass's body in another. Smaller separate pieces are Christ's hands and feet, and the legs, ears and tail of the ass. The belly of the ass is hollowed out. The unpainted base has four slots for wheels, and a hole for towing. The third finger of Christ's right hand is broken off. The grey paint is not original. There are traces of earlier pigmentation on Christ's face, and of a gold border on the robe. A bridle was formerly held in Christ's left hand.

Bequeathed by Captain H. B. Murray.

Sculptures of this kind – known as *Palmesel* – were made in south Germany for celebrating Palm Sunday, when they were led in procession through the streets (for this custom see: E. Wiepen, *Palmsonntagsprozession und Palmesel*, Bonn, 1903). The types usually are traditional, and most *Palmesel* were often refurbished, proverbially so: 'aufgeputzt wie der Palmesel acht Tag vor Ostern' (spruced up like a Palmesel eight days before Easter). Both these things make them difficult to date. The London figure is in a tradition deriving from a *Palmesel* carved in 1456 by Hans Multscher of Ulm for the great Benedictine house of SS Ulrich and Afra in Augsburg (M. Tripps, *Hans Multscher*, Weissenhorn, 1969, pls. 97–8). The Multscher figure, now in a Dominican convent, at Wettenhausen, was the model for a number of Swabian *Palmesel*; there are early examples in the museums of Ulm (K. Gerstenberg, *Hans Multscher*, Leipzig, 1928, figs. 88, 90) and Berlin-Dahlem (Inv. no. 8144). The London figure is substantially later than these and, though the head keeps close to Multscher's pattern, the soft curvilinear modelling of the lower drapery and the crisp carving of the ass's mane suggest a south Swabian sculptor well into the first quarter of the sixteenth century.

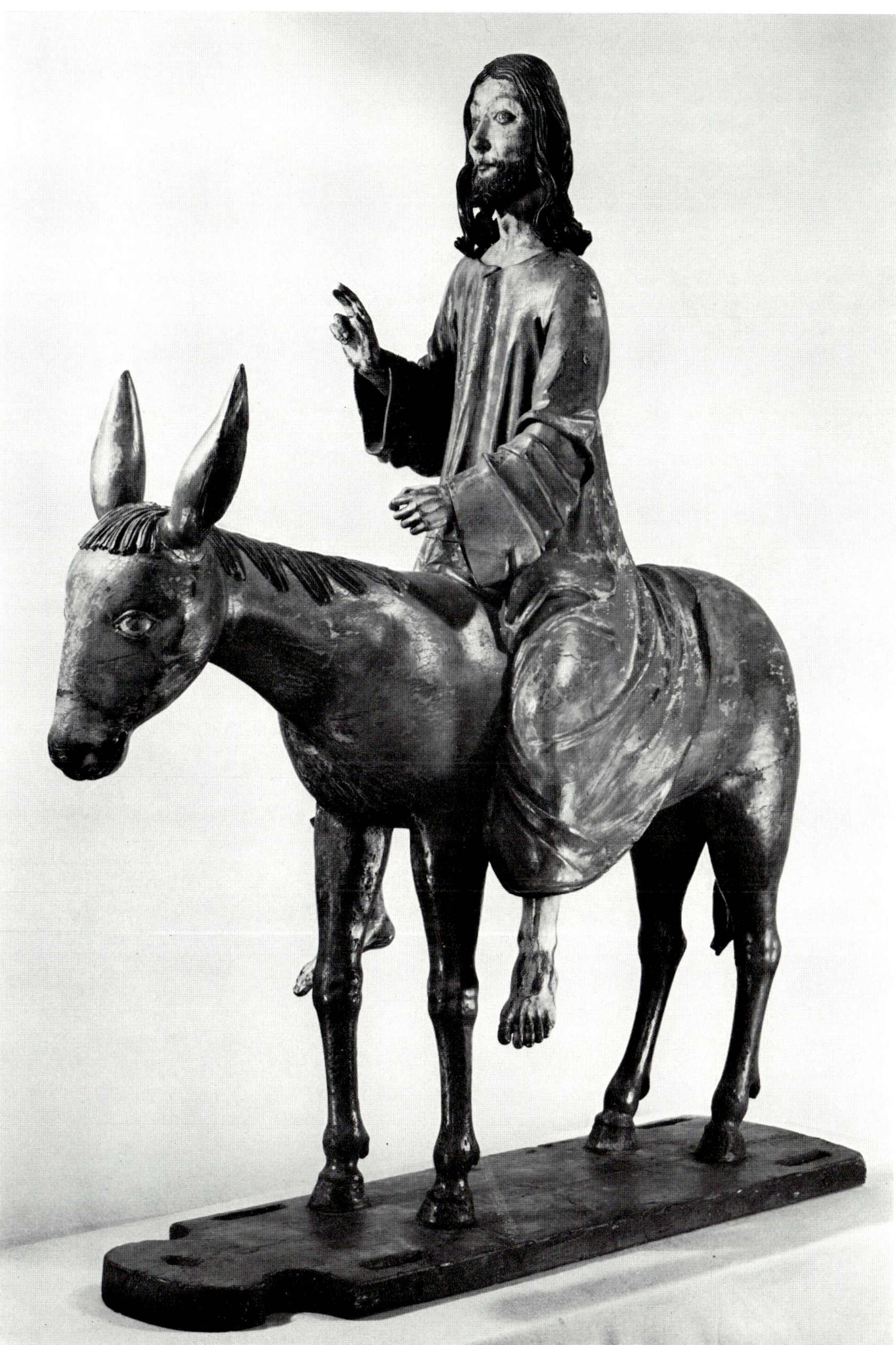

No. 6 WINGED RETABLE

Tirolese (Brixen). About 1500–10

Wood, painted. H. 14 ft 6½ in. (443·2 cm.).
Museum no. 192-1866

When the altarpiece is open, the sculptures displayed are as follows:
Left wing: The Annunciation (above) and the Presentation in the Temple (below).
Centre (left to right): St Florian, the Virgin and Child with Angels, St John the Baptist.
Right wing: The Nativity (above) and the Adoration of the Magi (below).
Predella: sculpture absent.

When the altarpiece is closed, the paintings displayed are as follows:
Left wing: St Corbinian and St Adalbert? (above) and St George and the Dragon (below).
Right wing: A Virgin Martyr and St Beatrice (?) (above) and St Martin and the Beggar (below).
Predella (left to right): St Barbara, St Dorothy, St Catherine and St Margaret.
Crowning shrinework and sculpture from above the *corpus* is lacking, as is the sculpture from the predella. There are many local losses and breakages in the foliate shrinework of the *corpus* and wings, and a number of detail losses in the sculpture, conspicuously in the hands and fingers. The paintings and also the polychromy of the sculpture have been extensively damaged and restored.

Bought in London, 1866 (Dr A. Salviati).

The retable is of a size to be from a high altar, not a side chapel, but suffers greatly from the loss of its crowning shrinework. It was acquired as Swabian, and this description was accepted by Julius Baum, who related it to the work of Ivo Strigel of Memmingen; it was later redesignated Tirolese. C. M. Kauffmann ascribes the paintings to the Tirol with a date round 1500, relating them to those on the altars from Tramin, now in the Bayerisches Nationalmuseum at Munich, and Tessenberg (A. Stange, *Deutsche Malerei der Gotik*, vol. x, Berlin, 1960, figs. 307–08, 309), and points to St Corbinian as a typically Tirolese subject. The Tramin altar is attributed on the basis of its sculpture and shrinework to Hans Klocker (T. Müller, *Bayerisches Nationalmuseum, München, Die Bildwerke in Holz, Ton und Stein 1450–1540*, Munich, 1959, pp. 81–7), active in Brixen in the period 1480–1500, and the sculpture of the London altar also relates closely to Brixen work. Gisela Scheffler associates the altar with a figure of the Virgin from Vals, now in the Diözesanmuseum at Brixen (Inv. no. 12), and sees it as a work from the Pustertal, east of Brixen, and mainly supplied from Bruneck. But the shrinework of the *corpus* is uniform with that of the high altar in

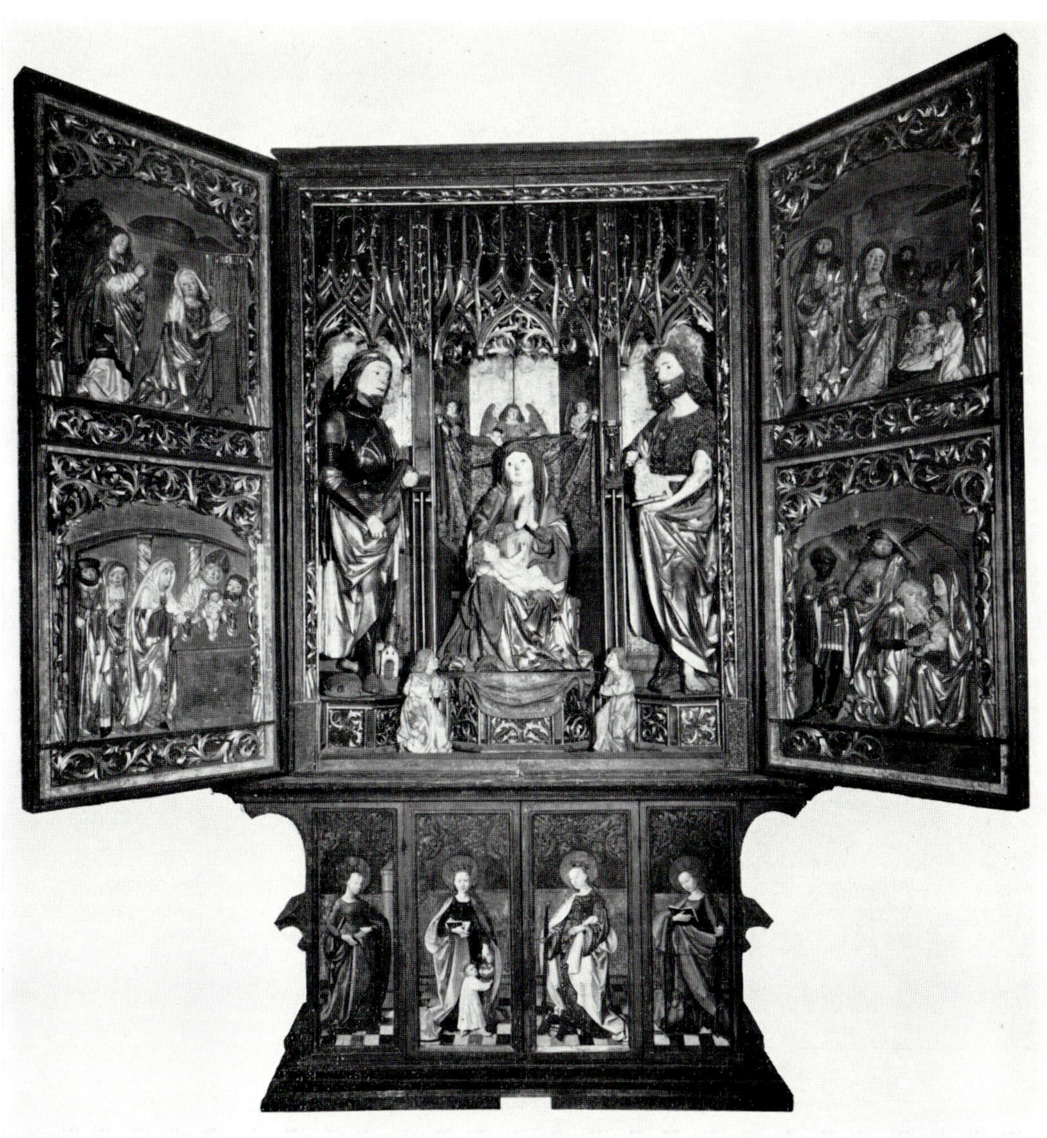

the church of SS Ingenuin and Albuin at Saubach in the Eisacktal (H. Semper, *Michel und Friedrich Pacher*, Esslingen, 1911, fig. 137), Brixen work of about 1500–10. The circumstances of the Tirolese sculpture trade – with large contractors such as Klocker using a changing range of painters, sculptors and joiners – discourage stylistic attribution to masters. The London altar is a work of about 1500–10 in the Brixen style and format, influenced by Hans Klocker; the sculptures of the altar are not consistent enough with those firmly associated with Klocker himself to argue an origin in Klocker's own shop.

J. Baum, *Altschwäbische Kunst*, Augsburg, 1923, p. 66; G. Scheffler, *Hans Klocker*, Augsburg, 1967, p. 89; C. M. Kauffmann, *Catalogue of Foreign Paintings in the Victoria and Albert Museum*, vol. i, London, 1973, no. 343.

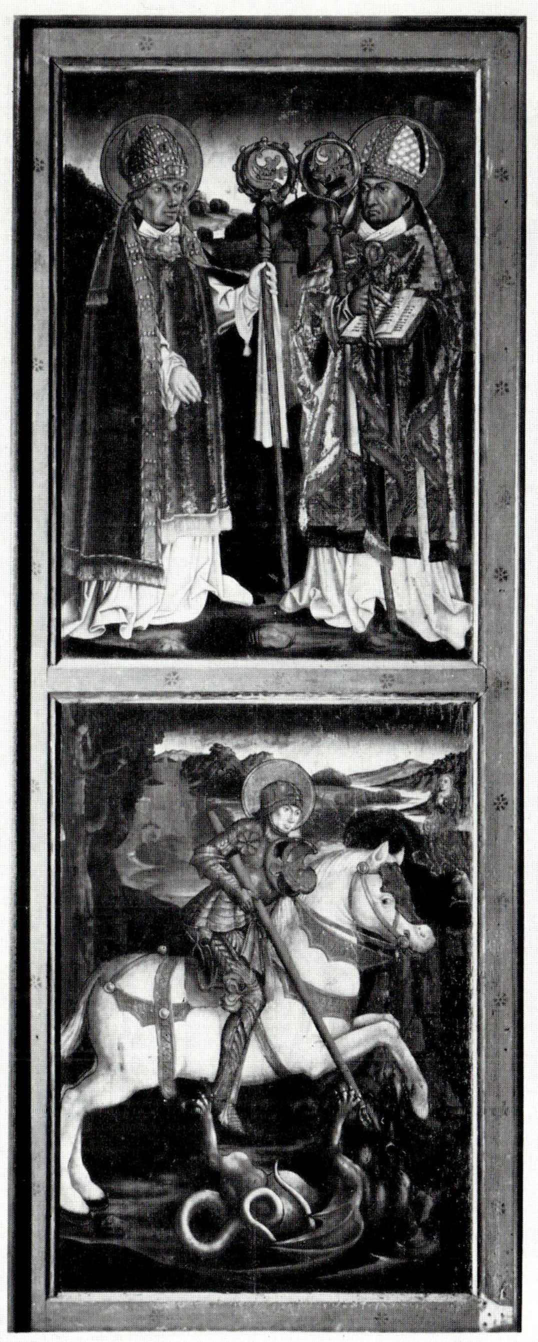

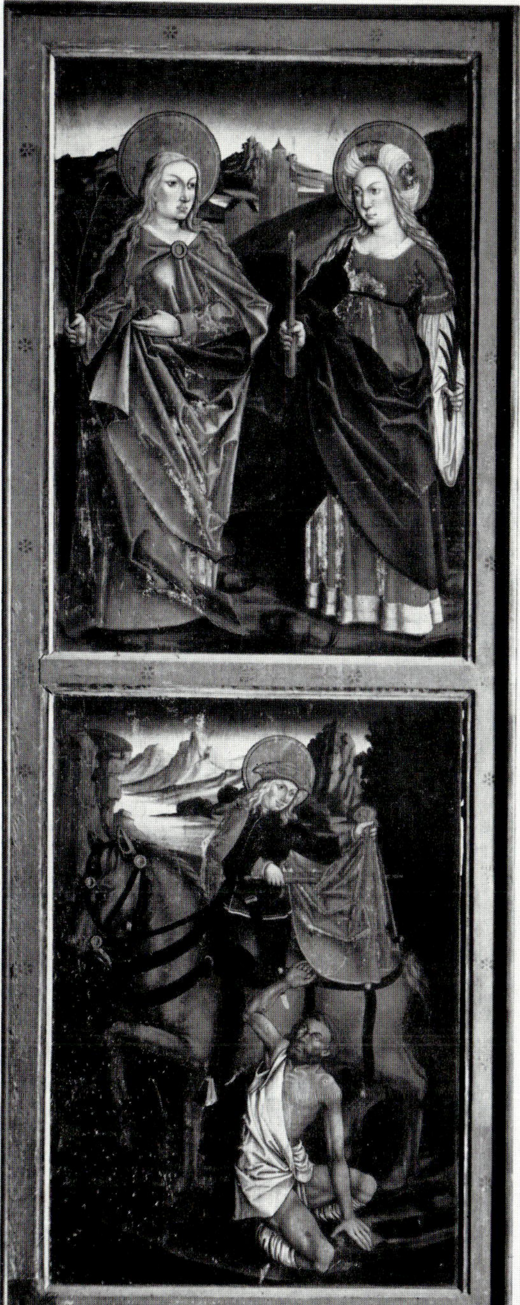

No. 7 THE VIRGIN AND CHILD

Austrian (Styria ?). About 1500–20

Limewood, painted. H. 2 ft 8¾ in. (83·2 cm.); w. 3 ft 0¼ in. (92·1 cm.). Museum no. A.13-1960

The fingers on the Child's left hand are broken, and the Virgin's left hand is restored. The pigmentation of the flesh is not original, but the remains of gilding over a red ground on the outer drapery and of ultramarine on the inner drapery probably are.

Given by Sir Thomas Barlow.

The group was formerly in the collection of Dr Richard Oertel, sold in 1913 (Sale Catalogue, Lepke, Berlin, 6–7 May 1913, p. 39, no. 144 & pl. 85). Professor T. Müller (personal communication) was told by Dr Oertel that he had obtained the figure from a dealer in Innsbruck, who in turn stated that it came from the district of Mariazell in Styria.

The Styrian provenance of the piece is not inconsistent with its style. The type of the Virgin, adapted to a squat shrine, is not uncommon in Austria and there are parallels for the idiosyncratic angels, kilted and short-haired, in the high altar of 1517 in the church of Waldburg, near Freistadt in upper Austria, for example (G. Tripp, 'Zur Restaurierung gotischer Schnitzaltären' in *Oesterreichische Zeitschrift für Kunst und Denkmalpflege*, vol. vii, 1953, fig. 130). More generally the rustic late gothic drapery, the chunkily blowing head-veil, and the bean-shaped heads, are found in both lower Austrian and Styrian work: see, for instance, the *Dürnberger Altar* of 1507 in the Stiftskirche at Seckan (K. Garzarolli von Thurnlackh, *Mittelälterliche Plastik in Steiermark*, Graz, 1941, pl. 97, and R. Kohlbach, *Steirische Bildhauer*, Graz, 1957, pp. 441–42).

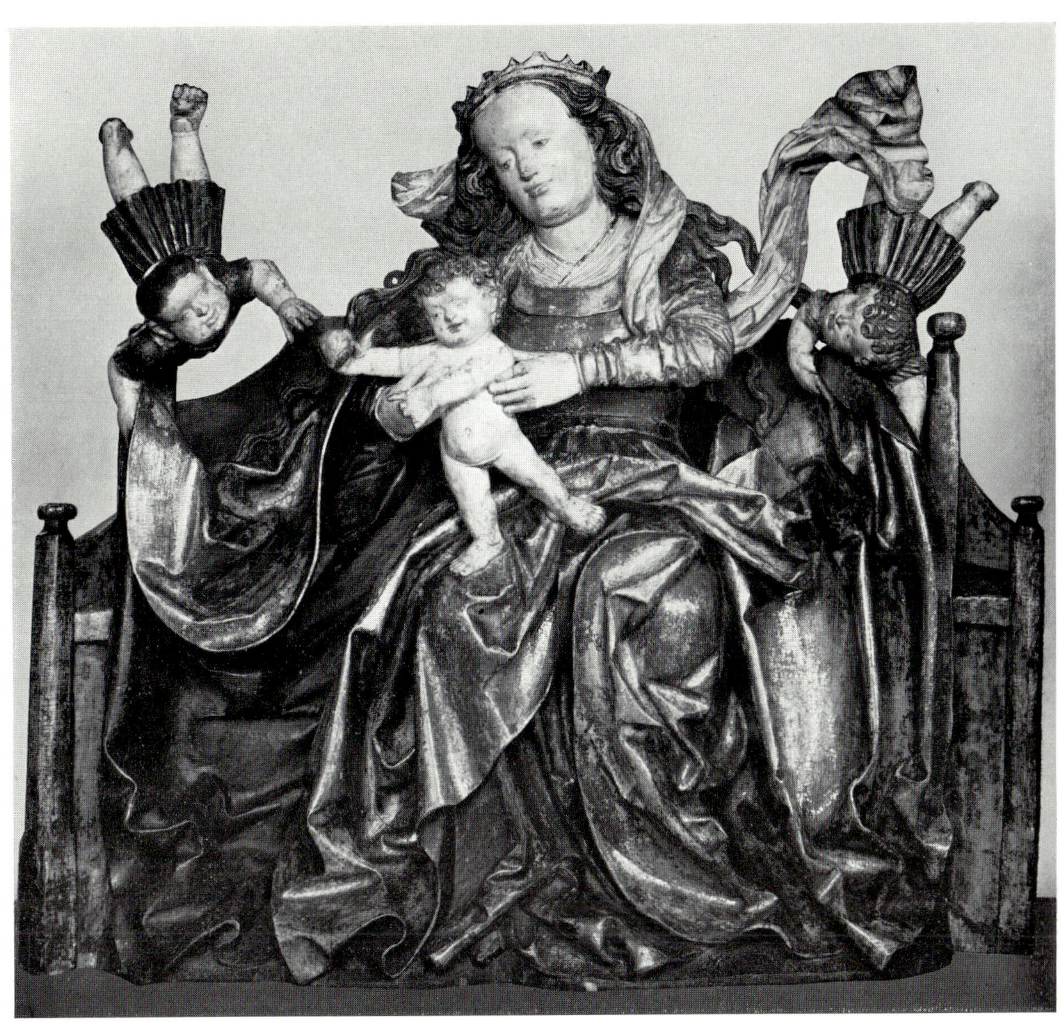

No. 8 WINGED RETABLE

Upper Rhenish (Strasbourg?). About 1510–20

Limewood, painted. H. 5 ft 2½ in. (158·8 cm.); w. 8 ft 1½ in. (247·7 cm.). Museum no. 125-1873

The back of the central panel is painted with foliage; on the backs of the wings are painted the Virgin and Child with St Anne. At the back of the frame is a branded mark 'L.F.P.M.' in two cartouches. Very extensively restored in 1934.

Bought in London, 1873 (Siegmund Stern). Vendor stated that it had been in the collection of Prince Pückler, presumably Hermann Fürst von Pückler-Muskau (1785–1871), and came from a church in Boppard-am-Rhein near Coblenz. In 1818 Hermann von Pückler-Muskau bought and removed from the Carmelite church in Boppard a quantity of the fifteenth century stained glass windows. It is possible that the retable was bought from the Carmelite church at the same time as the glass, but there is no direct evidence for this and it is also possible that the story of the glass, which had taken on some notoriety, was allowed to suggest an origin for the altarpiece.

This retable is of moderate size, suitable for a side-altar. If it were from the Carmelite church in Boppard (see above) its natural position would be on one of four massive square piers on the north side of the nave, facing west. The St Christopher and the Magdalen on the wings are after woodcuts by Dürer, both of about 1504 (A. Bartsch, *Le peintre graveur*, vol. vii, Leipzig, 1808, p. 136, no. 104 & p. 132, no. 84), the Magdalen being an adaptation of the Mary in the Visitation print of the *Marienleben* (fig. 6). The altar has been attributed to Martin Schaffner (b. 1478–79) of Ulm by Baum, Feulner and (more tentatively) Pinder; to Ulm but not to Schaffner by Otto; and to an Alsatian master by Sommer. No argument has been offered for the attribution to Schaffner, which would have to depend primarily on comparison with two reliefs from an altar formerly in Wettenhausen and now in Munich (T. Müller, *Bayerisches Nationalmuseum, München, Die Bildwerke in Holz, Ton und Stein, 1450–1540*, Munich, 1959, nos. 246-47). The attribution to an Alsatian master by Sommer is based on a comparison with the altar in the Spitalkirche at Bergheim near Rappoltsweiler (S. Hausmann, *Elsässische und Lothringische Kunstdenkmäler*, vol. i, Strasbourg, 1896, pl. 105). The similarities with Schaffner and with Ulm sculpture are in fact superficial. The relief drapery style and the head types derive from work done in the circle of Niclaus Hagenower of Strasbourg round the turn of the century. For the drapery, the hands, the head types of Joseph and Joachim, and the flattening of the floor in the foreground, compare the relief of twelve Apostles from an Assumption altar in the church at Saverne (Bas-Rhin), a piece from Hagenower's workshop in the early 1490s (Badisches

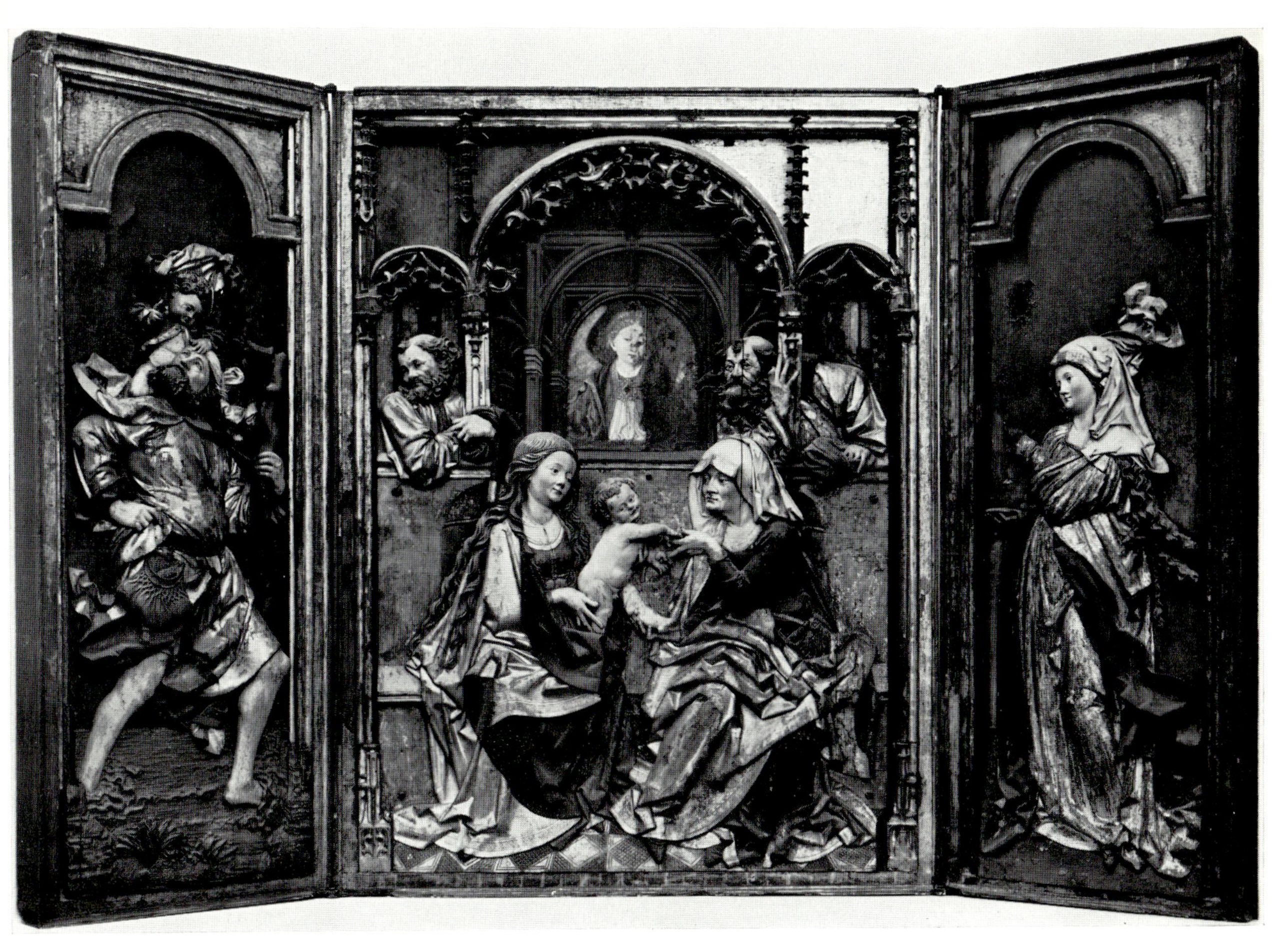

Landesmuseum, Karlsruhe, *Spätgotik am Oberrhein 1450–1530*, Karlsruhe, 1970, pl. 111).

W. Bode, *Geschichte der deutschen Kunst*, vol. ii, Berlin, 1887, p. 130; E. Stahl, *Die Legende vom Heiligen Riesen Christophorus*, Munich, 1920, vol. i, p. 197, vol. ii, pl. 38; J. Baum, 'Marienbilder des 16. Jahrhunderts' in *Das Schwäbische Museum*, 1926, p. 146; A. Feulner, *Die deutsche Plastik des 16. Jahrhunderts*, Munich, 1926, p. 60 & pl. 31; G. Otto, *Die Ulmer Plastik der Spätgotik*, Reutlingen, 1927, p. 267; C. Sommer, 'Zur Annaselbdritt-Gruppe des Nikolaus Gerhaert von Leyden' in *Berliner Museen*, vol. xlvii, 1927, pp. 112–14; W. Pinder, *Die deutsche Plastik vom ausgehenden Mittelalter bis zum Ende der Renaissance*, vol. ii, Berlin, 1929, p. 403; G. Tiemann, *Beiträge zur Geschichte der Mittelrheinischen Plastik um 1500*, Heidelberg, 1930, p. 18.

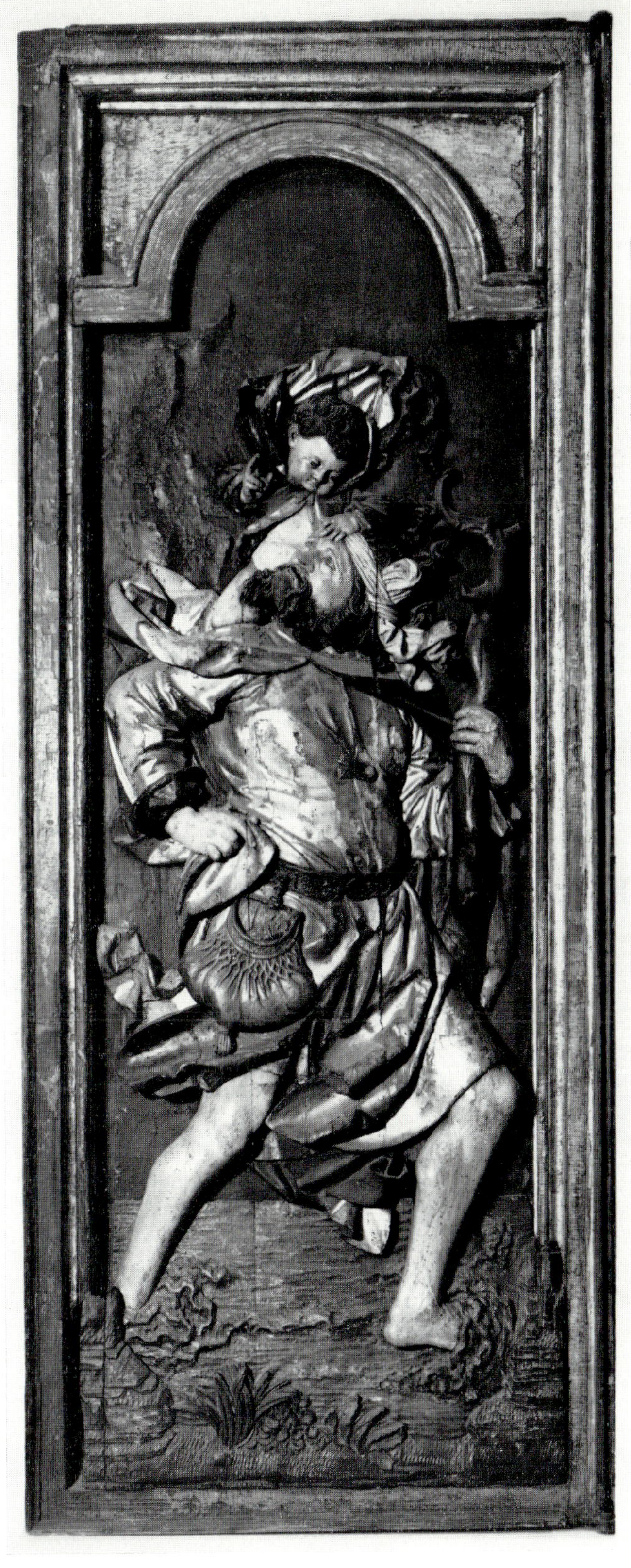

TILMAN RIEMENSCHNEIDER c. 1460–1531

Active in Würzburg from 1483, as a Master from 1485. His workshop at Würzburg was very large, and productive over a period of forty years; he made nineteen known retables, a number of which survive, and there is a quantity of stone sculpture after his designs. Retables still *in situ* are at St James's church at Rothenburg-on-the-Tauber (1499–1505) and at Creglingen (about 1505–08; fig. 2). Most of his work was monochrome. He died in 1531.

No. 9 KNEELING ANGELS

Tilman Riemenschneider c. 1460–1531
Franconian (Würzburg). About 1500

Limewood, formerly painted. H. 2 ft 1 in. (63·5 cm.), each figure.
Museum nos. A.16 & A.17–1912

Modern paint was removed from the figures at the time of their acquisition. They are made from composite pieces of wood, consisting of several small blocks joined together, and there are also a number of shallow surface cracks.

Bought from the church of the hamlet of Wolferstetten, near Külsheim in Baden, 1912. The figures were said to be originally from the church at Tauberbischofsheim, ten miles away, and plaster casts of the figures remained at Tauberbischofsheim. Weber states that the originals were transferred to Wolferstetten in 1771, and the church there is dated 1764.

The angels are designed as altar candlesticks, and need not be part of a retable complex. Though the paint removed from them on their acquisition by the Museum was certainly modern, they appear to have been intended for painting: the detail cutting of such features as eyes and fringes has the sharp coarseness used to counter the blurring effect of priming and paint. The figures are unmistakably work from Riemenschneider's shop, but represent a lower grade of quality than no. 10. The type of angel repeats that of the angels with the reliquary cross on the *Heiligblutaltar* at Rothenburg (1499–1505), and could have been made at any time between about 1490 and about 1510. They demonstrate the effective economy of carving developed in the delegated production of Riemenschneider's large workshop.

E. Tönnies, *Tilman Riemenschneider*, Strasbourg, 1900, pp. 272–73;
A. Weber, *Til Riemenschneider*, 3rd ed., Regensburg, 1911, p. 232;
H. Schrade, *Tilman Riemenschneider*, vol. ii, Heidelberg, 1927, p. 32;
M. von Freeden, *Tilman Riemenschneider: Leben und Werk*, 3rd ed., Munich, 1965, p. 35.

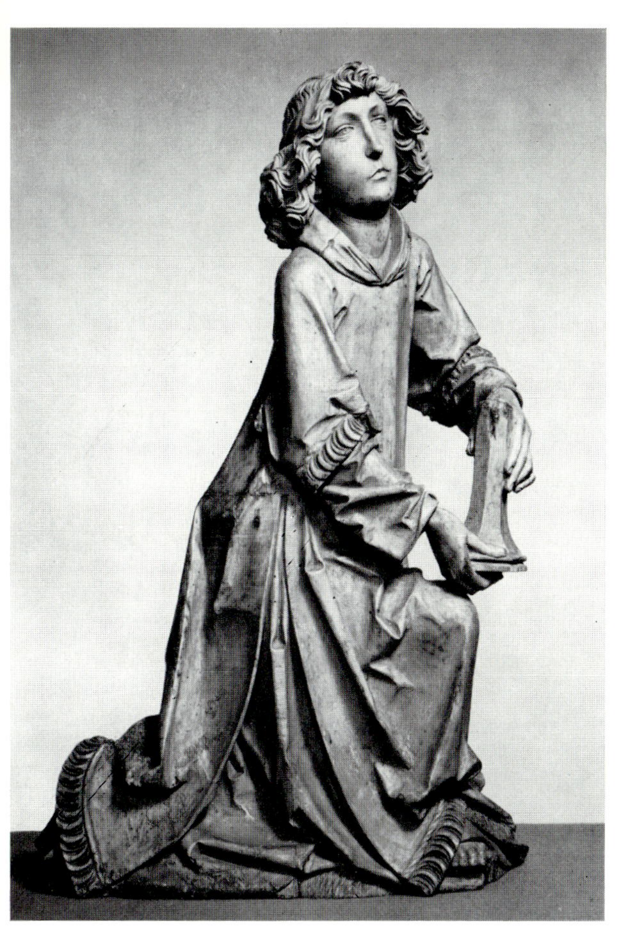

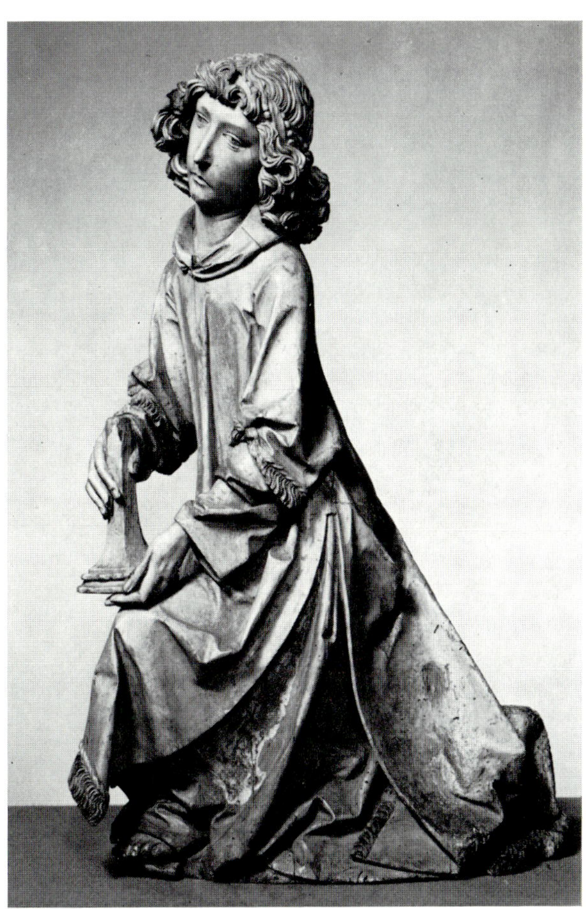

No. 10 MARY SALOME AND ZEBEDEE

Tilman Riemenschneider c. 1460–1531
Franconian (Würzburg). About 1520

Limewood, glazed. H. 3 ft 11 in. (119·4 cm.); w. 1 ft 7½ in. (49·5 cm.). Museum no. 110-1878

Written on the back of the group: 'ANNO. 1500. gemacht. /1817. Ren'. The group has been heavily restored along the base, and the lower left section of the bench has been replaced. These repairs and also the dark glaze probably date from the restoration of 1817.

Bought from a French dealer in 1878.

The group is a fragment from the right side of a larger group of the Holy Kindred (for whom see no. 15) and its pair, from the left side, with Mary Cleophas and Alphaeus, is in the Öttingen-Wallerstein collection at Harburg. These two groups demand a centre-piece between them, to include St Anne, her three husbands, the Virgin, St Joseph and the Christ Child. A third fragment, a group of St Anne and her husbands, now in a private collection in Tiefenbrunn, is of about the same height and in a similar style, but is considerably less deep (about 12 cm. as opposed to about 20 cm.). Winzinger has persuasively argued that this is part of the lost centre-piece. He postulates a winged retable in which the central section or *Corpus* was correspondingly shallower than the wings: there are no analogies for such a retable, and the unequal depths are more probably due to the demands on space of a fully modelled background in the *Corpus*. The attribution of the London and Harburg groups to Riemenschneider has never been in dispute. There is also general agreement that the lost retable from which they come must be a relatively late work, though quite how late is uncertain. Riemenschneider was active at least until 1527, but the chronology of his later work has not been firmly plotted. The very late date proposed by Winzinger, after 1525, is less likely than the end of the second decade of the century, a little before or contemporary with the sandstone altar in the church at Maidbronn near Würzburg (about 1519–23).

E. Tönnies, *Tilman Riemenschneider*, Strasbourg, 1900, pp. 237–38; A. Weber, *Til Riemenschneider*, 3rd ed., Regensburg, 1911, pp. 270–71; H. Schrade, *Tilman Riemenschneider*, vol. i, Heidelberg, 1927, pp. 173–74; J. Bier, *Tilman Riemenschneider: Die reifen Werke*, Augsburg, 1930, pp. 47–8; T. Demmler, 'Ein unbekannter Riemenschneider' in *Pantheon*, vol. xiv, 1932, p. 209; F. Winzinger, 'Ein zerstörtes Hauptwerk Tilman Riemenschneiders' in *Das Münster*, vol. iv, 1951, pp. 129–37; W. Paatz, *Süddeutsche Schnitzaltäre der Spätgotik*, Heidelberg, 1963, p. 93.

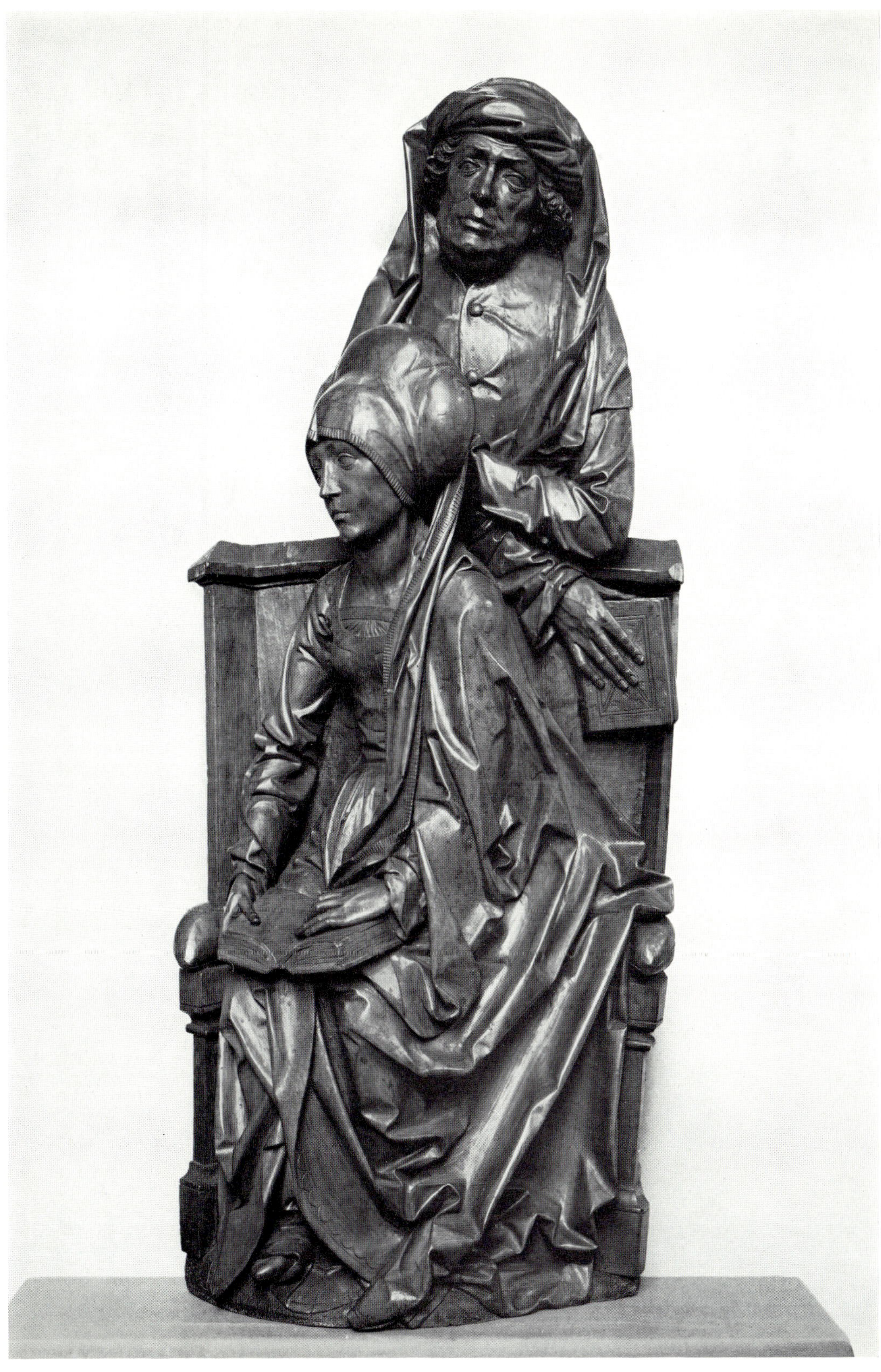

No. 11 THE VIRGIN MARY, ST JOHN AND ST MARY MAGDALEN

Upper Saxony (Zwickau?). About 1510

Limewood, painted and gilded. H. 2 ft 7 in. (78·7 cm.); w. 1 ft 11 in. (58·4 cm.).
Museum no. 50-1864

The group is carved from three joined pieces of wood. The Magdalen's right hand is missing; the thumb and index finger of the Virgin's right hand are broken. Much of the paint has flaked, exposing the gesso beneath.

Bought in Munich, 1864 (Otto Entres).

The weakness of the carving towards the left edge of the group suggests it was designed to be masked here by framing shrinework. It is a fragment of a Crucifixion group, probably from the centre-piece of a small retable. Voegelen, who treats the relief as Swabian, has pointed out that the composition resembles designs of the school of Rogier van der Weyden; on the other hand, the carving involves face types and drapery patterns of a generally north Franconian character. Though sculptures combining these elements occur in the middle Rhineland, the particular analogies for the London group come rather from the work in Upper Saxony of Peter Breuer, journeyman in Riemenschneider's shop in 1492 and Master in Zwickau by 1502. For the general style of the relief composition, compare the Nativity in Hartmannsdorf and the Annunciation from Niedercrinitz now in the Stadtmuseum at Freiberg (W. Hentschel, *Peter Breuer*, 2nd ed., Dresden, 1952, figs. 104, 101); for the type of St John, see the St John at Schönau (Hentschel, *op. cit.*, fig. 77). The motif of the Magdalen's hood, hanging down to a terminal flourish, is a regular mannerism of Breuer's work: for example, the central figures of the retables from Callenberg and Dobia (Hentschel, *op. cit.*, figs. 87–8). An attribution by Habicht to the Master of the High Altar in the Johanniskirche at Osnabrück is not persuasive.

M. Voegelen, 'Die Gruppenaltäre in Schwäbisch Hall und ihre Beziehungen zur niederländischen Kunst' in *Münchner Jahrbuch der bildenden Kunst*, vol. xiii, 1923, pp. 126–29; V. C. Habicht, *Niedersächsische Kunst in England*, Hanover, 1930, pp. 103–06, fig. 87.

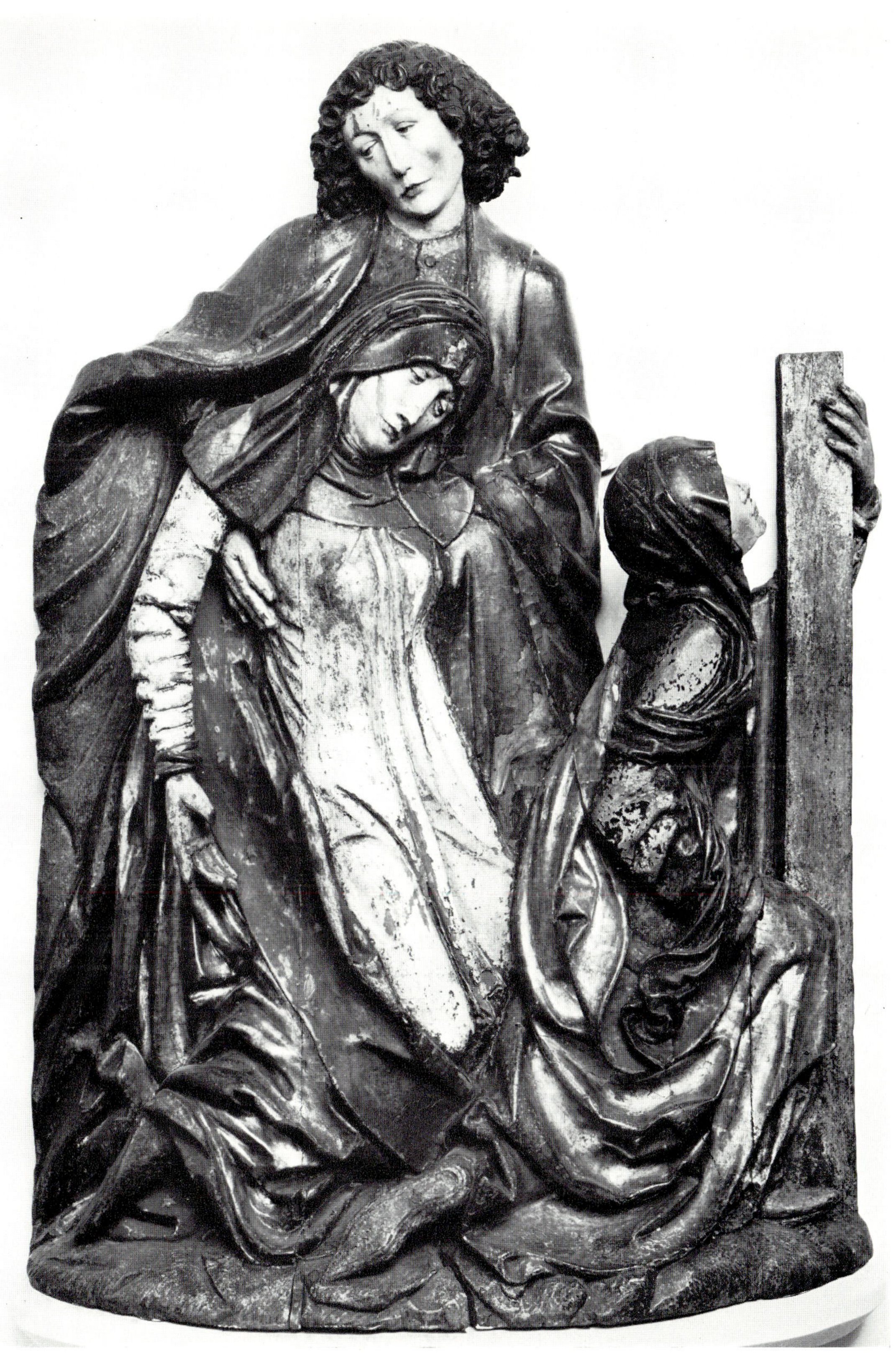

No. 12 A SAINT

Franconian (Eichstätt?). About 1500–10

Limewood, painted. H. 5 ft 2½ in. (158·8 cm.); w. 1 ft 10 in. (55·8 cm.). Museum no. A.24-1921

The fingers of the right hand and the feet with their support are broken off. The paint is not original, but the gilding of hood and mantle probably represents the original colouring.

Given by Mrs E. A. Abbey.

Without the attribute formerly held in the figure's broken left hand the subject cannot be identified. The present pigmentation of the drapery – gold mantle and hood, maroon tunic with a white fringe, black scapular – does not fit any of the orders wearing a habit of these four garments, of whom the most important were the Dominicans and Carmelites. The figure is from the wing of a retable altar and is remarkable for the monumental effect contrived with the lowest relief: the modelling of the drapery at no point rises above 2¼ inches from the baseboard. The design is generally mid-Franconian, and in a number of ways relates to carving done in Eichstätt during the first twenty years of the sixteenth century. The sustained sinuous line of the edge of the mantle, the effect of crushed glazed fabric made by the short, straight, angled folds within this edge, and the play of these against the long, straight, vertical folds of the tunic and scapular, all recur often in Eichstätt work: see, for example, the Virgin in the Convent of St Walburg, the Man of Sorrows group in the Mariahilfkirche at Berching, the Virgin and other figures in the retable of the church at Treuchtlingen (illustrated in F. Mader, 'Der Meister des Eichstätter Domaltares' in *Die Christliche Kunst*, vol. ix, 1912–13, pp. 213–38, in figs. on pp. 220, 222, 232).

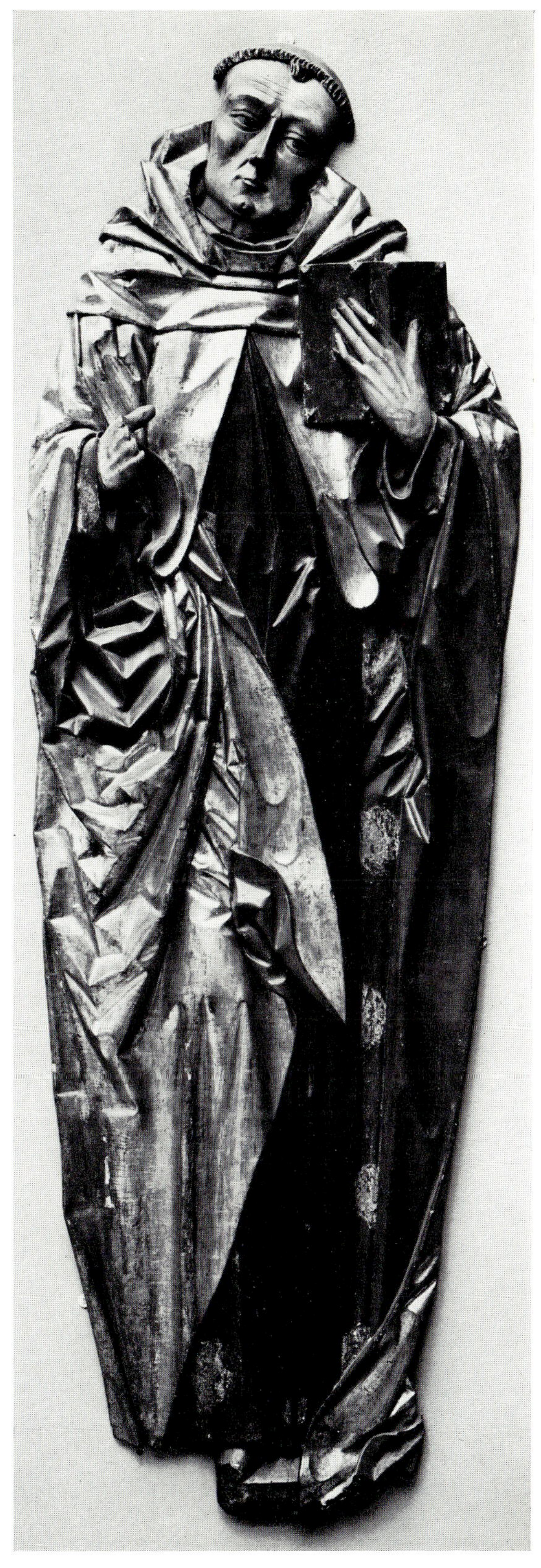

VEIT STOSS c. 1447–1533

Veit Stoss was born in about 1447 in Swabia and worked at first in Nuremberg. In 1477 he went to Cracow for nearly twenty years: his main works there were a massive retable for the Marienkirche and a red marble tomb for King Casimir IV. In 1496 he returned to Nuremberg and spent most of the rest of his career there: dated works in Nuremberg are the Volckamer memorial in St Sebaldus (1499), the *Englische Gruss* in St Lorenz (1517–18), and an altar intended for the Carmelite church (1520–23) but now in Bamberg cathedral. Stoss's Nuremberg workshop seems to have been not very large. He died in 1533.

No. 13 THE VIRGIN AND CHILD

Veit Stoss c. 1447–1533
Franconian (Nuremberg). About 1520

Boxwood. H. 8 in. (20·3 cm.).
Museum no. 646-1893

A section including the Virgin's forearm and the Child's left arm is carved separately; and a small wedge has been made good by inlay in the front fold of the Virgin's cloak. There are traces of a gilt edging about 2 mm. wide round the whole of the cloak, and a rather narrower one round the edge of the head veil. There are also traces of gilding on the inside of the crescent moon and at the neck of the Virgin's gown. The ends of two locks of hair and part of the Virgin's right little finger are broken off. There are a number of fine vertical cracks.

Bought in London (Christie's, 12 June 1893, no. 31) from the Field collection. In the possession of George Field in 1862, when it was exhibited at the Special Loan Exhibition, South Kensington (*Catalogue*, rev. ed., 1863, p. 578, no. 6742).

The figure is the only secure example of a statuette by Stoss, but small virtuoso pieces of the kind were probably a conspicuous part of his later work; a figure of Christ, a span or so long (about 25 cm.) and valued at 40 florins, is singled out for praise by Neudörfer (Johann Neudörfer, *Nachrichten von Künstlern und Werkleuten* [1574], ed. Lochner, Vienna, 1875, p. 84). The attitude, with the Child held high out to the right and balanced by the Virgin leaning to the left, derives from Upper Rhenish types, but is here given an unusual pert accent by removing its original motivation; without the usual tilt of the Virgin's head to the Child or the Child's movement towards the Virgin, both address themselves directly to the beholder. The attribution to Stoss was first made by Voss in 1908 on the basis of comparison with the *Hausmadonna* now in the Germanisches Museum at Nuremberg, and has not been disputed. Dates suggested have

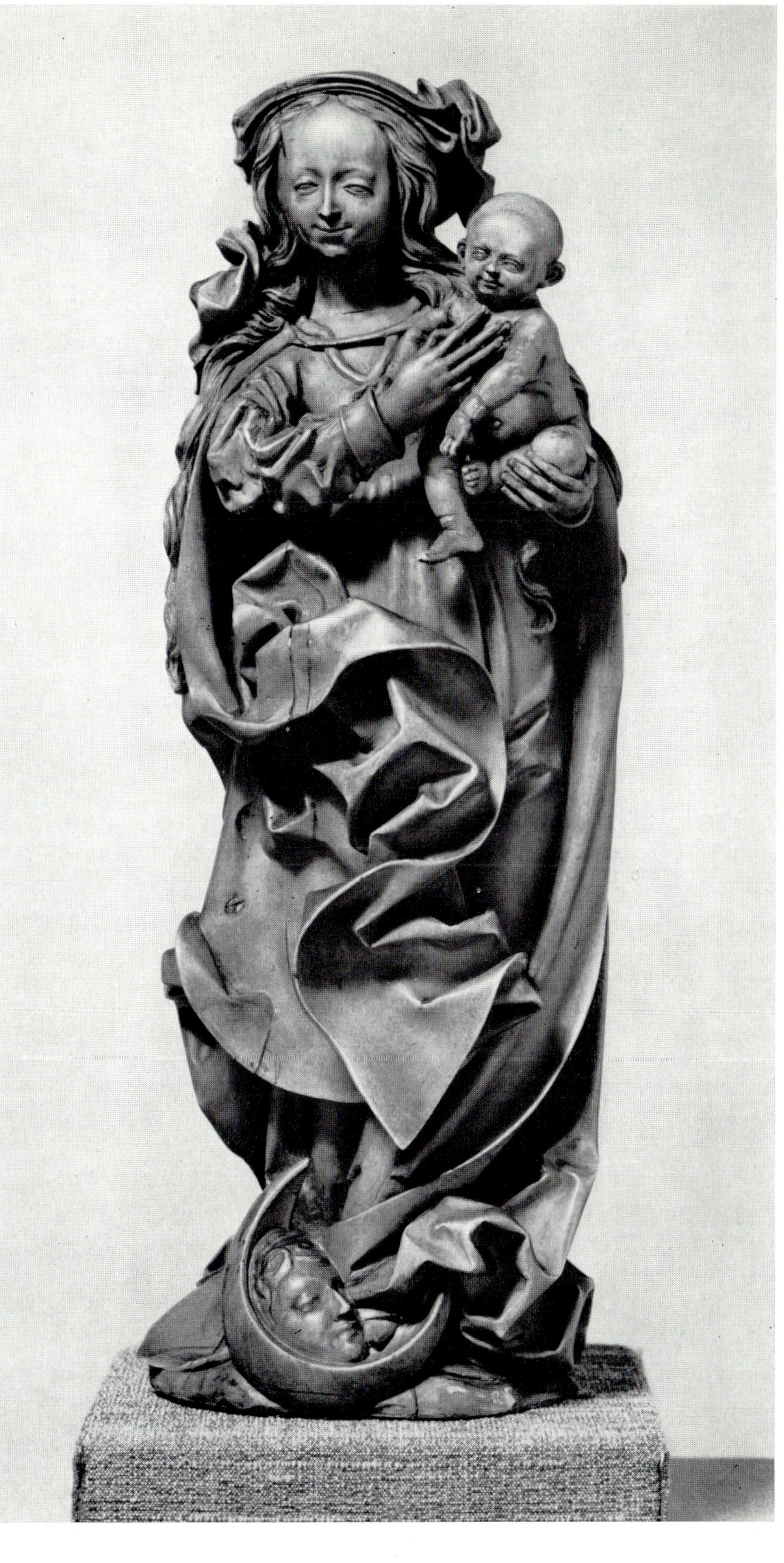

ranged from 1510 (Dettloff) to about 1520–23, contemporary with the retable now in Bamberg Cathedral (Voss, Daun, Müller). The uncertain chronology of Stoss's later work, and also the probability that in such virtuoso pieces he was under pressure to provide work in his established style, make close dating impracticable; but quite a late date is likely.

H. Voss 'Eine Madonnenstatuette des Veit Stoss im South Kensington Museum' in *Repertorium für Kunstwissenschaft*, vol. xxxi, 1908, p. 258; M. Lossnitzer, *Veit Stoss*, Leipzig, 1912, p. 128; B. Daun, *Veit Stoss und seine Schule*, Leipzig, 1916, pp. 139–40; E. Lutze 'Die "Italienischen" Werke des Veit Stoss' in *Pantheon*, vol. xix, 1937, p. 188, and *Veit Stoss*, Berlin, 1938, p. 38; T. Müller in Thieme-Becker, *Künstler-Lexikon*, vol. xxxii, 1938, pp. 131–38; H. Stafski, *Anzeiger des Germanischen Museum, 1936–9*, p. 132; S. Dettloff, *Wit Stosz*, vol. i, Wrocław, 1961, pp. 161–62; T. Müller, *Sculpture in the Netherlands, Germany, France and Spain, 1400–1500*, Harmondsworth, 1966, pp. 24, 183.

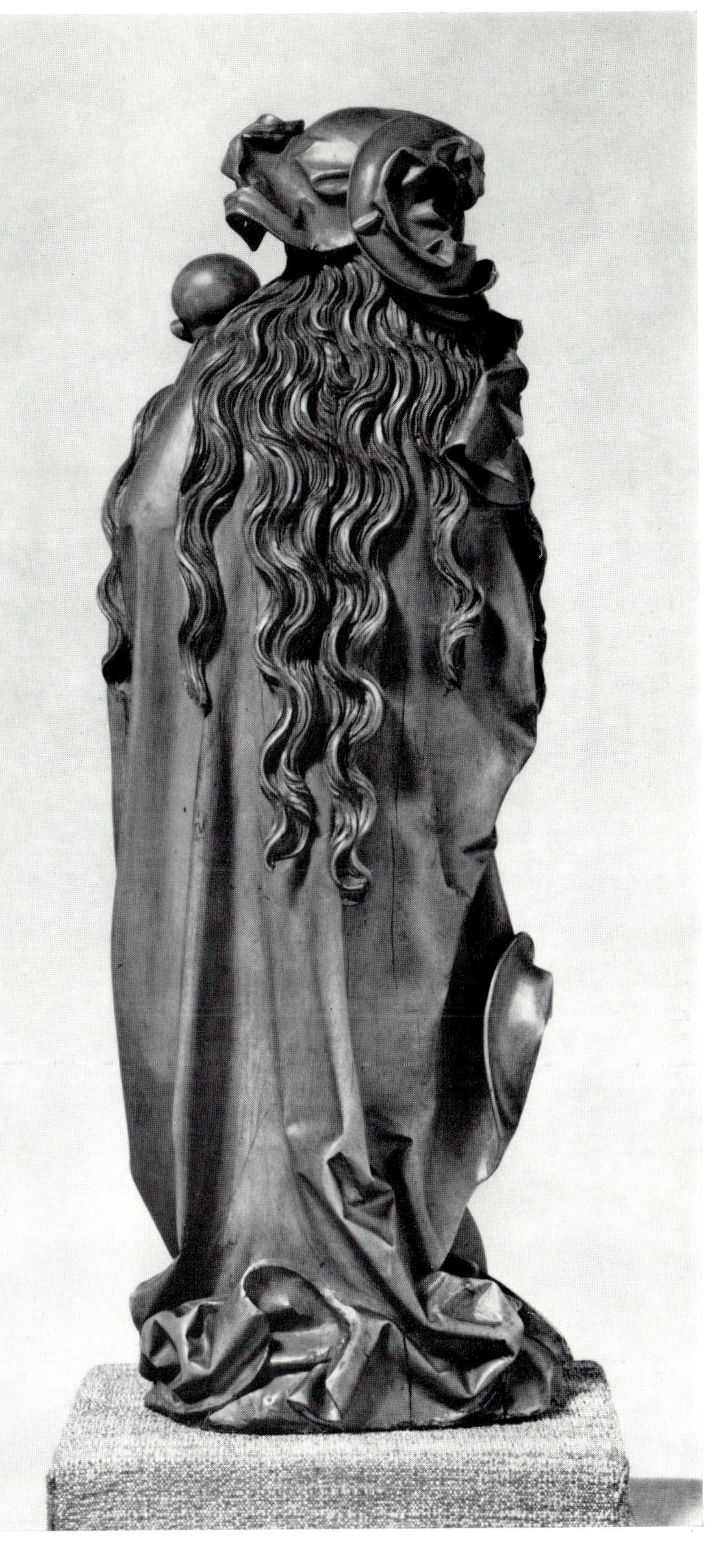

No. 14 THE VIRGIN AND CHILD

Bavarian. About 1520

Limewood, painted. H. 3 ft $9\frac{1}{4}$ in. (114·9 cm.).
Museum no. A.21-1941

A crown is missing from the Virgin's head, and some locks of hair are broken off at the bottom. The polychromy appears to be baroque.

Bought in London, 1941 (W. F. Ohly) under the Bequest of Captain H. B. Murray.

The figure is seriously unbalanced by the loss of its crown. It is one of very many of the period deriving at a distance from the y-shaped drapery motifs of Hans Leinberger of Landshut, but it is not of his immediate school. The rod-like folds and flourishes on the hem have close parallels in work associated with the Master of the Rabenden Altar, an apparently prolific contemporary of Leinberger working in the upper Inn valley: see the St Sebastian in Munich (J. Rohmeder, *Der Meister des Hochaltars in Rabenden*, Munich, 1971, fig. 27, the most recent study of the Master). The head type of the Virgin and a number of details, such as the carving of the hair and the out-thrust left foot, also fit this style; the river-god posture of the Child, popularized by the Erharts' altar at Blaubeuren, occurs in work from the Rabenden master's school (see the altar of 1517 from Unterölkofen in T. Müller, *Bayerisches Nationalmuseum, München, Die Bildwerke in Holz, Ton und Stein 1450–1540*, Munich, 1959, p. 234). The stylistic division of minor Bavarian sculpture into a number of anonymous masters (for which, see particularly, O. Bramm, 'Hans Leinberger, seine Werkstatt und Schule' in *Münchner Jahrbuch der bildenden Kunst*, vol. v, 1928, pp. 116–89) is conventional and due for review.

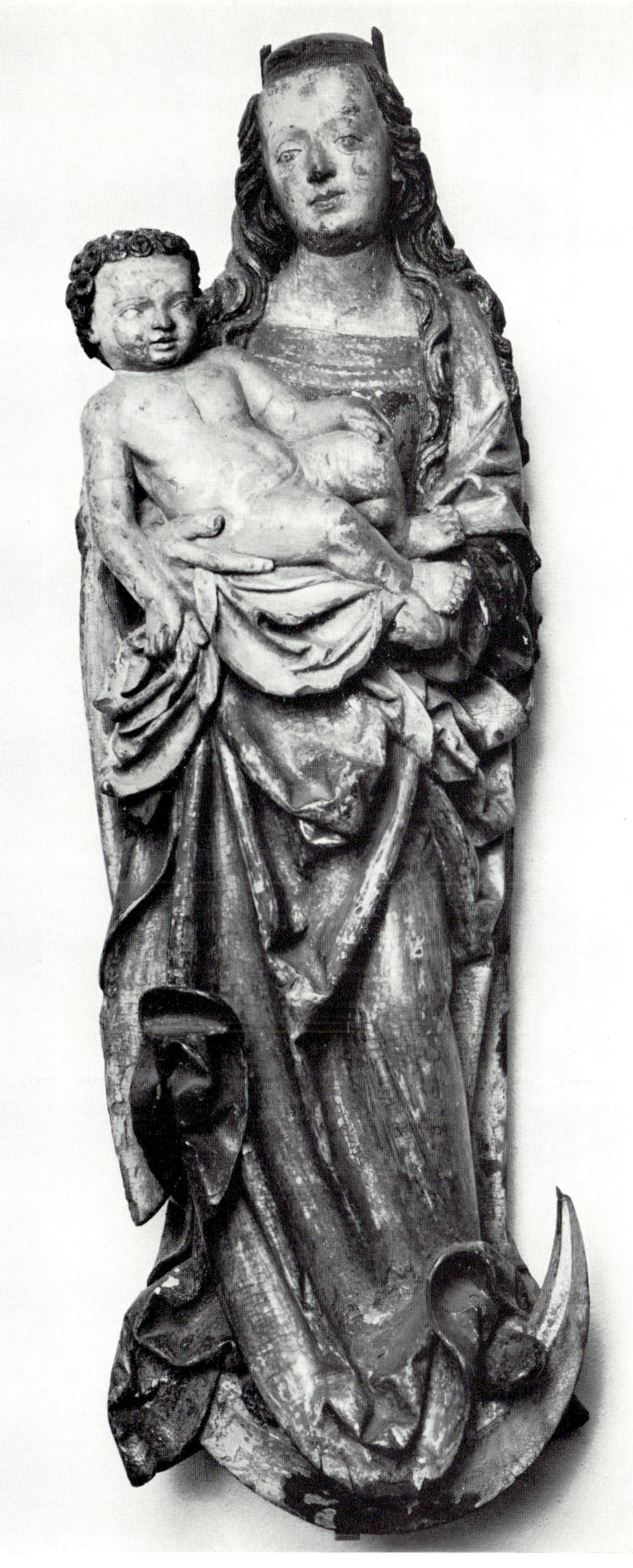

No. 15 THE HOLY KINDRED

Swabian (Memmingen?). About 1525

Limewood, painted. H. (centre group) $6\frac{3}{8}$ in. (16·2 cm.).
Museum no. 573-1872

When acquired, the carvings were housed in a frame apparently adapted from a baroque desk drawer. Modern paint was removed in 1931.

Bought in Nuremberg, 1872 (A. Pickert).

This series of three reliefs is from a small domestic or travelling altar. The Holy Kindred were a popular subject in fifteenth and early sixteenth century art (see also no. 10): they refer to the legendary three daughters of St Anne by her three husbands, Joachim, Salomas and Cleophas, and originate in a vision of the Blessed Colette Boilet in 1408. In the central group The Virgin and St. Anne sit with the Child; behind them Joseph leans forward, and the three husbands of St Anne stand at the back. In the left group is Mary Cleophas with her husband Alphaeus and four children – James the Less, Joseph the Just, Simon and Jude. In the right group are Mary Salome and Zebedee, her husband, with their two children – John the Evangelist and James the Great. For the iconography of the Holy Kindred see K. Künstle, *Iconographie der christlichen Kunst*, vol. i, Freiburg im Breisgau, 1928, pp. 331–32. The reliefs are attributed to the Master of the Mindelheim Sippe by Theodor Müller. This sculptor is one of two principal masters distinguished among a large group of south Swabian sculptures in the 'parallel fold style'. The Master of the Mindelheim Sippe is named after a group of the Holy Kindred (*Sippe*) in the Liebfrauenkapelle at Mindelheim; the other, the Master of Ottobeuren, is named after carvings in the Benedictine abbey at Ottobeuren. Both would be active in the 1520s and 1530s, but the Mindelheim master is considered the elder of the two. The terms were established by Karl Gröber, *Schwäbische Skulptur der Spätgotik*, Munich, 1922, and the *œuvres* were reviewed by Luise Böhling in the *Jahrbuch der preussischen Kunstsammlungen*, vol. 58, 1937, pp. 26–39, 137–52; more recently, however, Alfred Schädler has argued that both *œuvres* were produced in one large workshop, probably in Memmingen ('Das Werk des "Meisters von Ottobeuren"' in *Ottobeuren 764-1964: Beiträge zur Geschichte der Abtei*, Augsburg, 1964, pp. 136–52). The London carving certainly belongs in the Mindelheim/Ottobeuren group of sculptures. It is closest to an Adoration of the Magi of 1520–25, which was formerly in Berlin (Inv. 461. Destroyed 1945), and which is usually attributed to the Mindelheim master.

T. Müller in *Das Schöne Allgäu*, vol. xiii, 1950, p. 206.

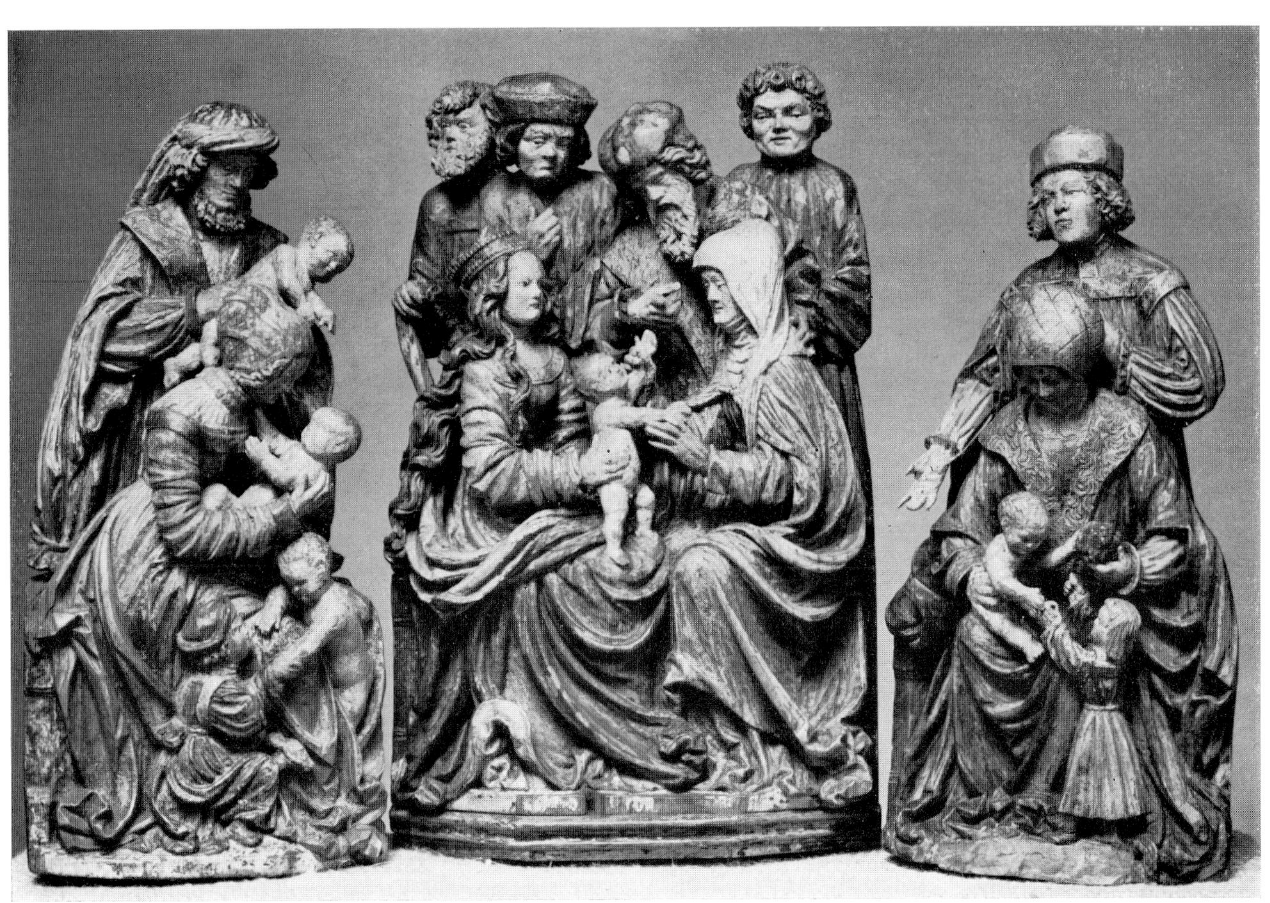

HANS DAUCHER c. 1485–1538

Son of the *Kistler* (cabinet-maker) Adolf Daucher, who married Gregor Erhart's sister and worked in Augsburg from 1491. Hans was an apprentice in Erhart's shop from about 1500 and became a Master in Augsburg in 1514. Until about 1522 he was probably in partnership with his father, and their works include a Lamentation group in the church of St Anne in Augsburg (finished by 1518) and the high altar of St Anne's church in Annaberg in the Erzgebirge (finished 1521): the relative contributions of Adolf and Hans are debatable. Adolf died in 1522/23 and Hans's later works are mainly small-scale. He died in 1538 in Stuttgart.

No. 16 ST JOHN

Hans Daucher c. 1485–1538
Swabian (Augsburg). About 1523

Limestone. H. 2 ft 8 in. (81·3 cm.).
Museum no. 49-1864

A section is broken off at bottom right, including the left hand of the demi-man in the crest. There are a number of small chips on the figure.

Bought in Munich, 1864 (Otto Entres).

The figure is evidently the mourning John from a Crucifixion group. The arms at his feet – Quarterly, 1 and 4 a griffin rampant against a rock; 2 and 3 two halberds crossed in saltire. Crest: a demi-man supporting [in his sinister hand a crown surmounted by a griffin and] in his dexter hand a halberd – are those of Lamparter von Greiffenstein (J. Siebmacher, *Grosses und allgemeines Wappenbuch*, vol. vi, pt 2, 1891–1911, p. 177). Lieb has drawn attention to a letter, dated 21 August 1524, from Ritter Hans Lamparter von Greiffenstein at Augsburg to Kaspar Nützel the Elder at Nuremberg in which he states (a) that an epitaph he has been having made in Augsburg for his father Dr Gregorius Lamparter von Greiffenstein (d. 1523) with a view to erection in Nuremberg is now finished; (b) that it contains figures of the Crucified Christ, Mary, St John, St Gregory and Gregorius Lamparter kneeling before them; (c) that he has heard that the city fathers at Nuremberg have in mind to do away with images, and he is disinclined to send a fine sculpture to Nuremberg if it is liable to destruction by headstrong people (*mutwillig Leut*). He would therefore like to be informed about the situation before deciding whether or not to dispatch it. There is no sign of the monument having been erected in Nuremberg, and the presumption is that the St John is a fragment from it. The figure was attributed to Adolf Daucher by Kris, who noted its close relation with the Daucher altars in Augsburg and Annaberg. Karl Feuchtmayr (in Lieb, pp. 457–58) ascribed it rather to

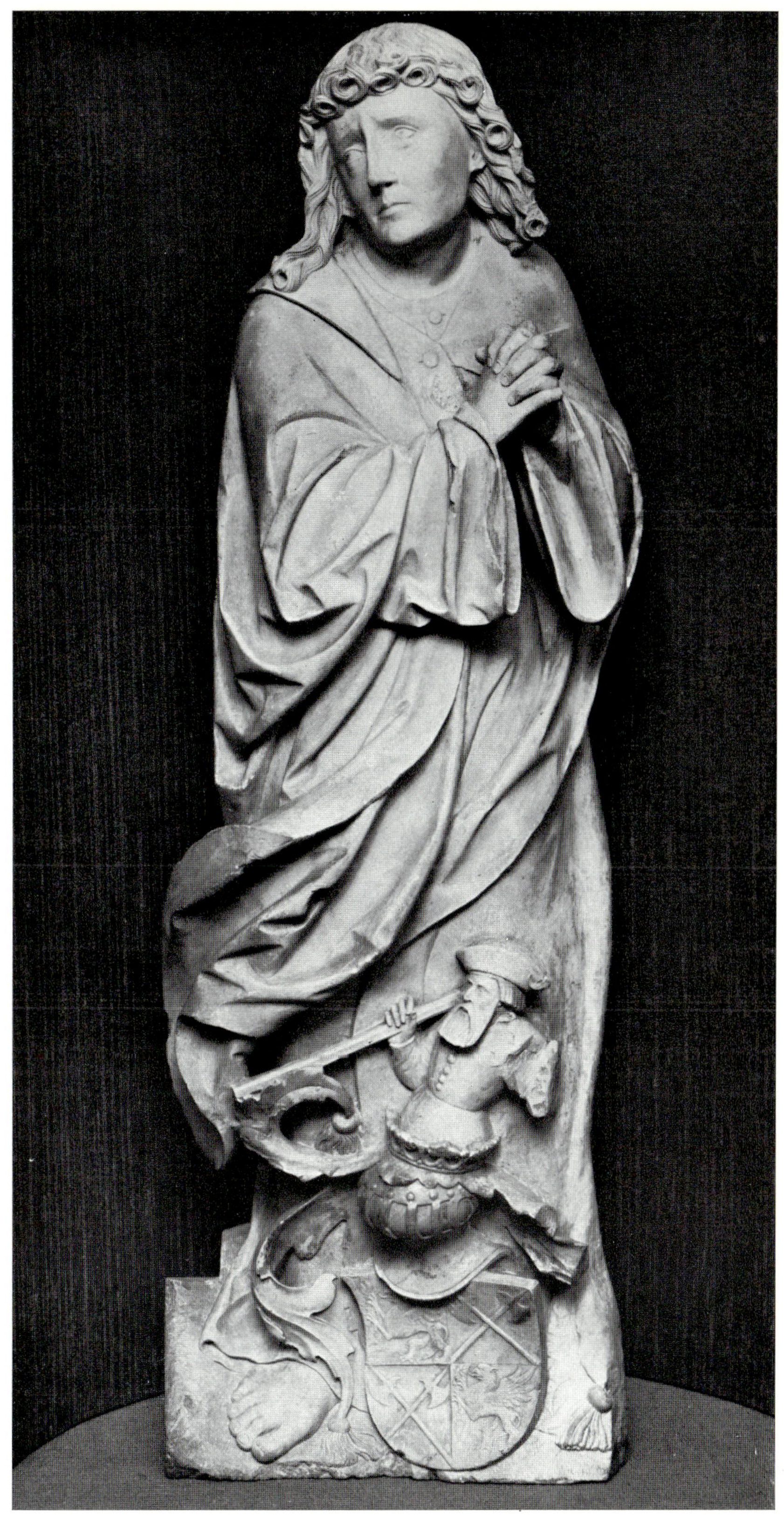

Hans Daucher, the son of Adolf. He argues both from the fact of the Hans Lamparter letter suggesting a date (1523–24) after Adolf's death (1522–23), and from general indications that the role of Adolf, who was not a member of the sculptors' guild, was much less important in the Dauchers' sculpture than was previously thought. Both arguments are persuasive.

E. Kris, 'Notizen zu Adolf Daucher' in *Beiträge zur Geschichte der deutschen Kunst*, vol. ii, 1928, pp. 433–36; N. Lieb, *Die Fugger und die Kunst im Zeitalter der Spätgotik und frühen Renaissance*, Munich, 1952, pp. 218, 249, 395, 457–58; A. Feulner and T. Müller, *Geschichte der deutschen Plastik*, Munich, 1953, fig. 261.

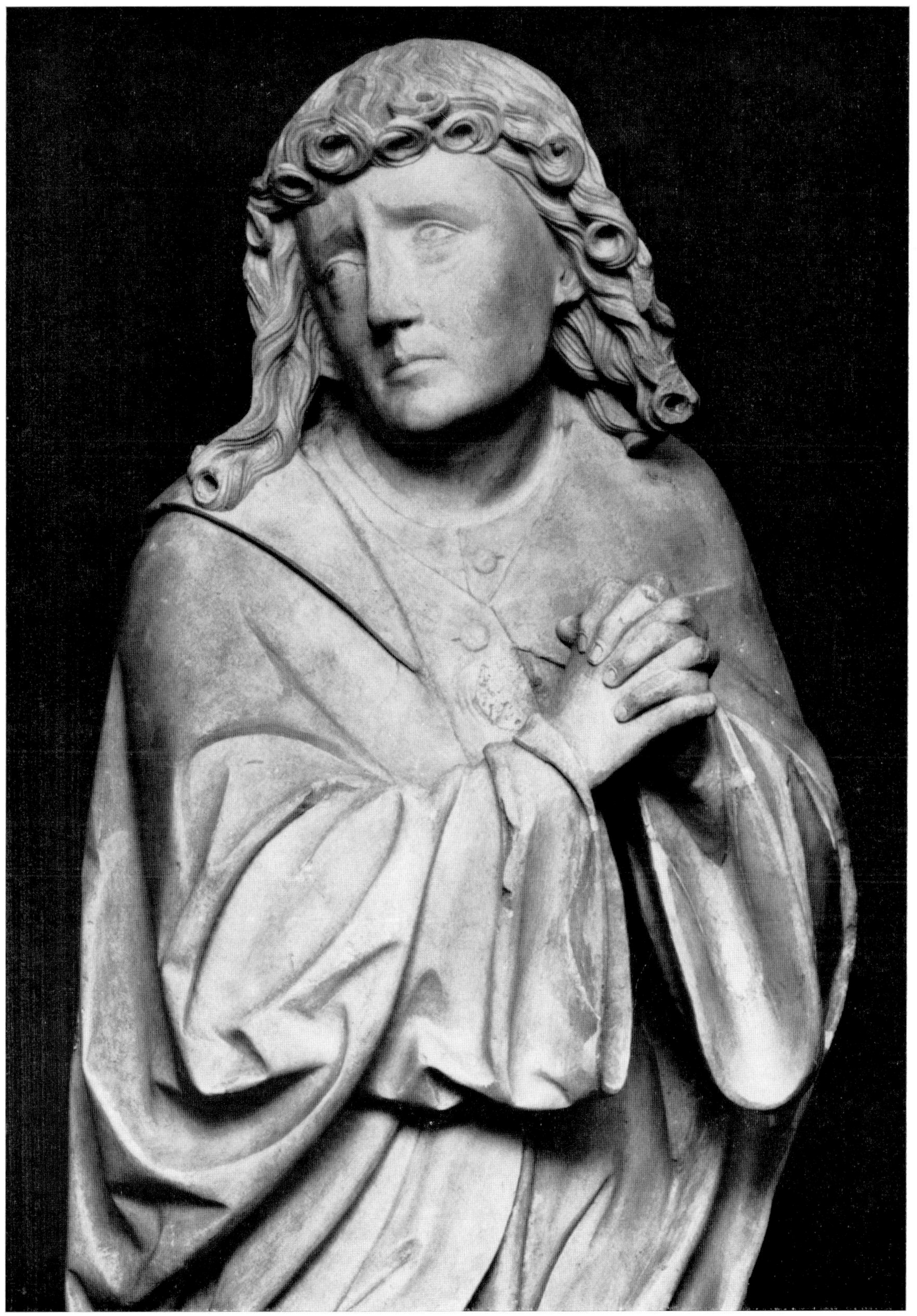

No. 17 THE TAKING OF CHRIST

Swabian (Augsburg). About 1525

Solnhofen limestone. H. 1 ft 7⅞ in. (50·5 cm.); w. 1 ft 7⅞ in. (50·5 cm.). Museum no. A.41-1947

A number of cracks run across the right half of the relief, which is backed by a slab of reddish slate-like stone, and two sections, that above the heads of the three figures on the left and that comprising the half-figure on the extreme right, are additions in a slightly yellower stone.

Bought in London, 1947 (F. A. Drey), under the Bequest of Capt. H. B. Murray. Formerly in the collection of Sir Francis Cook, Doughty House, Richmond.

The composition is that of The Taking of Christ from Dürer's woodcut in the *Small Passion* (fig. 4), published in 1511 (A. Bartsch, *Le peintre graveur*, vol. vii, 1808, p. 119, no. 27), with the addition of an armed figure on the extreme right. The relief was published in 1954 in the *Burlington Magazine* with an ascription to the school of Hans Daucher and, in particular, to the sculptor of the altar reliefs in the Fugger Chapel of St Anna, Augsburg. However, the rectilinear drapery style, the angular relief cutting and the head types are not compatible with the manner of the Fugger Chapel reliefs or that of the group of reliefs signed by Hans Daucher; and an Augsburg master rather outside the circle of Daucher must be involved. The head types of Christ and Judas, the vein patterning on feet and hands, the formulas used for grasses and certain other details are repeated in a more evolved form in the reliefs associated with the Susanna and the Elders in Berlin (Inv. 2004), signed by Viktor Kayser (d. 1552/23), and it is in this tradition of Augsburg limestone sculpture rather than that of Daucher that A.41-1947 belongs. A relief of Christ carrying the Cross in the Germanisches Museum at Nuremberg (Inv. Pl.O.2070) most nearly approaches its style. Two things make attribution of such Augsburg reliefs hazardous. There are several masters shown by tax or guild records as in a substantial way of business to whom no works have yet been attributed: Viktor Kayser's master Jakob Murmann (1467–1546) is one of these. Further, joint workshops were common in Augsburg: Murmann, for instance, worked from the same premises as Loy Hering and Hans Daucher at different times. The London relief represents Kayser's starting point, perhaps simply the class of Augsburg sculpture from which he developed; but it may be a work from Murmann's shop in the period 1516–25, when Kayser was apprentice and journeyman.

'Museum Acquisitions' in *Burlington Magazine*, vol. xcvi, 1954, p. 129.

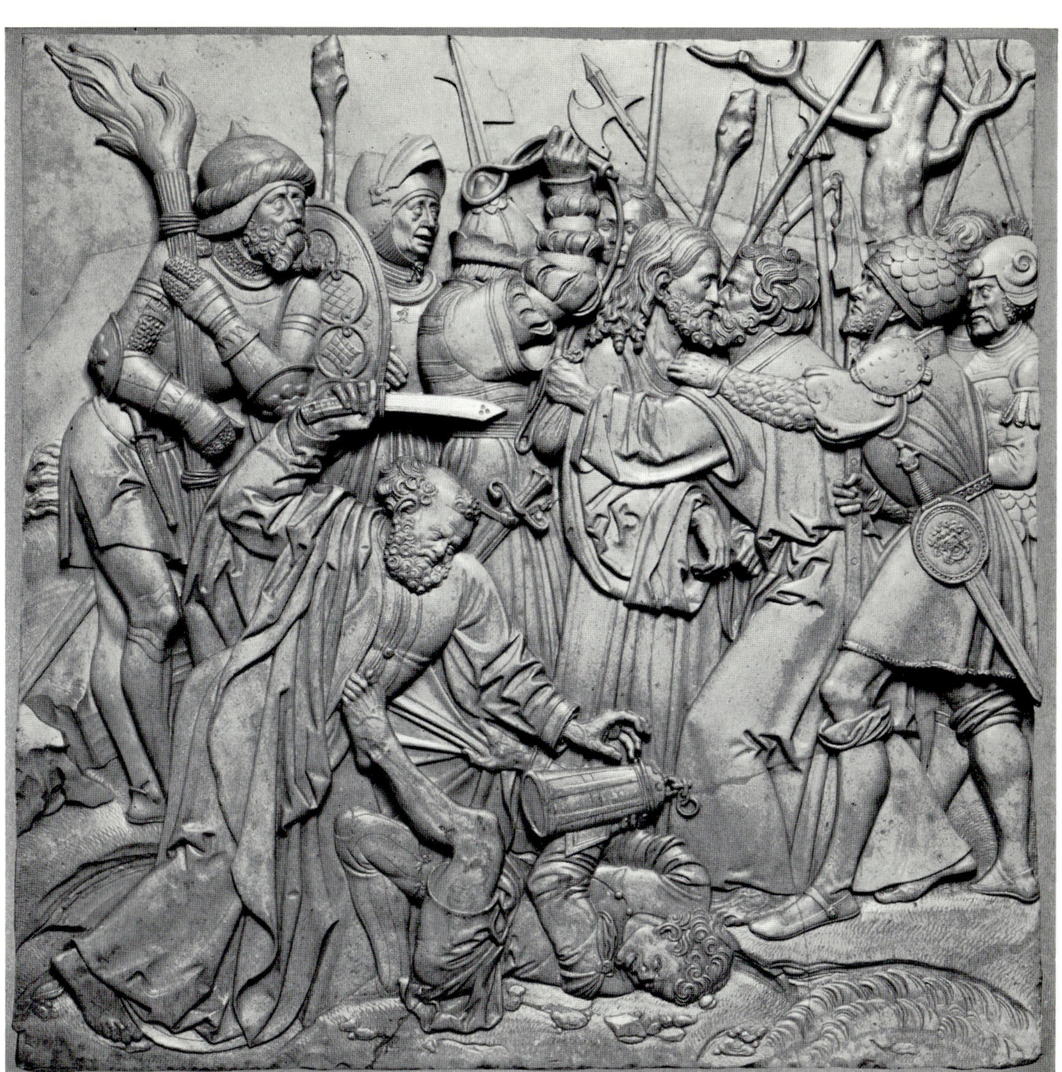

LOY HERING c. 1485–1555

Loy (i.e. Eligius) Hering entered the workshop of the Augsburg marble sculptor Hans Peuerlin or Baierlein the Elder (d. 1508) as an apprentice in 1499. From 1513 he was in Eichstätt, where his workshop was active for the next forty years; he eventually became Burgomaster of Eichstätt. The greater part of his production consisted of limestone epitaph reliefs of a type influential in southern Germany until the end of the century. Attribution of smaller narrative reliefs to Hering depends primarily on a signed Garden of Love in Berlin.

No. 18 THE FALL

Loy Hering c. 1485–1555
Franconian (Eichstätt). About 1520–30

Solnhofen limestone. H. 1 ft $3\frac{1}{4}$ in. (38·7 cm.); w. 10 in. (25·4 cm.). Museum no. 427-1869

A natural flaw in the stone slants upwards from Eve's left foot across Adam's legs. Bought in London, 1869 (Brooks).

The composition derives from a woodcut by Hans Baldung Grien (fig. 5) dated 1511 (A. Bartsch, *Le peintre graveur*, vol. vii, Leipzig, 1808, p. 306, no. 3). This print uses the dramatic device of setting a large serpent and its tree in the right of the picture plane, in advance of the figures of Adam and Eve. This motif is omitted from the sculpture, which is remarkable for its combination of low and full relief. A much smaller serpent appears behind the figures' heads. The reduction of Baldung's design, the unusual format, and the makeshift serpent are all accounted for by a natural flaw in the stone, running from Eve's left foot across Adam's legs, which would have emerged in the course of cutting. The group is given to Loy Hering by Bange, Grossman and von der Osten: the head types of Adam and Eve, the figure type of Eve, and the formulas for trees and foliage recur in Hering's signed Garden of Love in Berlin. The style of the Garden of Love is related in date by Bange to the epitaph of Wilhelm von Mur (d. 1536) in the church at Bergen near Neuburg an der Donau; but the similarities are very general, and the London carving is unlikely to date from later than 1530.

E. Bange, *Die Kleinplastik der deutschen Renaissance in Holz und Stein*, Florence/Munich, 1928, pl. 20a; City of Manchester Art Gallery, *German Art 1400–1800*, Catalogue by F. Grossman, 1961, p. 29; G. von der Osten and H. Vey, *Painting and sculpture in Germany and the Netherlands 1500–1600*, Harmondsworth, 1969, p. 258 & fig. 242; P. Cannon-Brookes, 'Loy Hering and the Monogrammist D. H.' in *Apollo*, vol. xciv, no. 113, July 1971, p. 46.

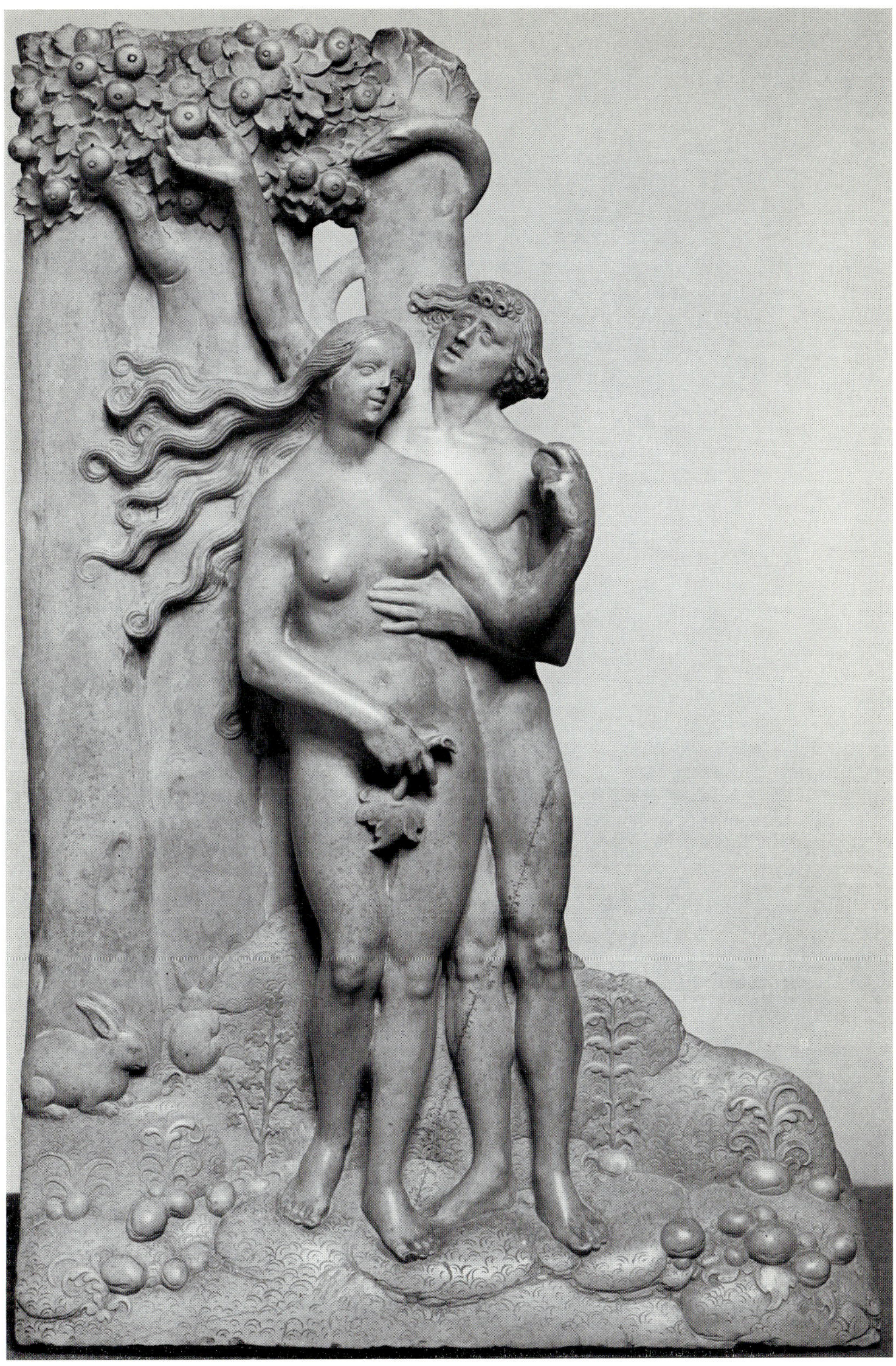

FRIEDRICH HAGENAUER active 1525–44

A native of Strasbourg, where he was trained and practised as a sculptor, Hagenauer appears to have worked in his earlier years as a medallist in Speyer, Worms, Mainz, Frankfurt, Heidelberg, Nuremberg, Passau and Salzburg. In 1525–27 he was in Munich, in 1527–32 in Augsburg. From 1533 he was active in Swabia and on the Upper Rhine, and from 1536 until 1544 in Cologne; later he may have been in the Netherlands. Hagenauer was one of the most productive of the sixteenth century German medallists; attribution of larger-scale work to him is problematical.

No. 19 THE VIRGIN AND CHILD

Friedrich Hagenauer; active 1525–44
Swabian (Augsburg). About 1530

Solnhofen limestone. H. 1 ft 5$\frac{1}{16}$ in. (43·3 cm.); w. 12$\frac{1}{2}$ in. (31·7 cm.).
Museum no. 7957-1862

A small segment at the bottom left has been broken off and reset. Around the heads of the Virgin and Child are five drilled holes for supporting some sort of nimbus. Gilding described as modern was removed from the columns in 1932. There are traces of gilding and a ground on the hair of the Virgin and Child, on the crown, on the fringe of the cloth-of-honour, on the raised foliation and mouldings of the architecture, and on alternate tiles of the pavement. There are traces of red pigmentation on the mouth of the moon. The painted arms are not original; examination under ultra-violet light shows traces of earlier arms underneath, too fragmentary to be identified. Cracks in the upper part of the relief, caused by an accident in 1968, are practically invisible from the front.
Formerly in the Soltikoff collection (*Catalogue des objets d'art et de haute curiosité composant la célèbre collection du Prince Soltykoff*. . . . Hôtel Drouot, Paris, 8 April 1861, p. 72, no. 251).

This relief is in a genre established by Hans Daucher in a series of small limestone reliefs of the Virgin in an Italianate hall; examples survive in Vienna (1518), Augsburg (1520) and Frankfurt (undated). The London relief is ascribed by Theodor Müller to a master working in Hans Daucher's manner around 1530–35. Its architecture is an exact copy of the background of Hans Burgkmair's woodcut portrait of the Emperor Maximilian (fig. 3), dated 1518. (A. Bartsch, *Le peintre graveur*, vol. vii, Leipzig, 1808, p. 211, no. 32). The type of the Virgin and the hard, round style of cutting are not characteristic of Augsburg; there is also a discrepancy between the virtuosity of minute carving and some clumsiness in the general design and placing of the figure. The design seems a curiously *retardataire* essay in Upper Rhenish patterns of about 1500–10.

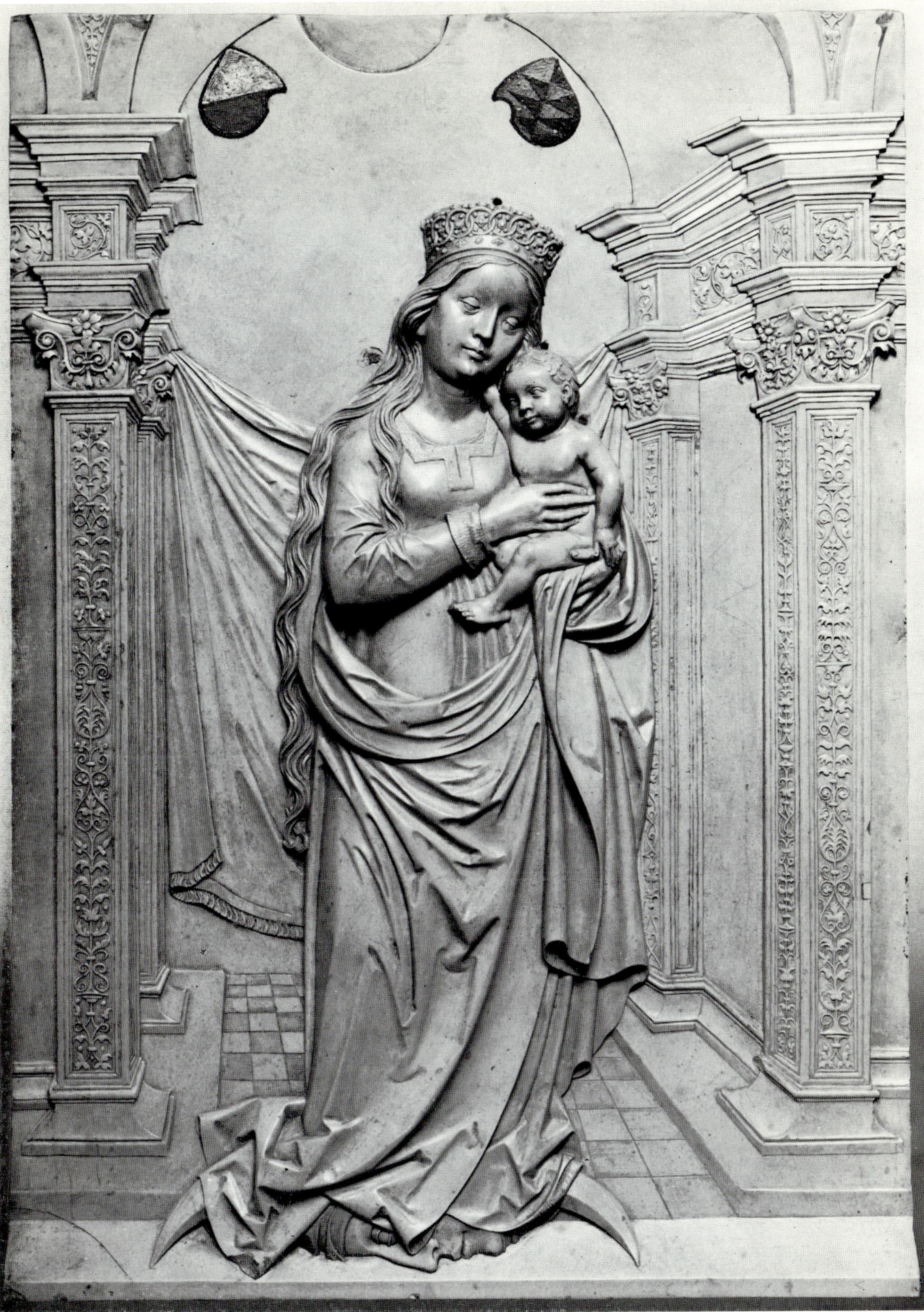

For the head-type of the Virgin, compare the St Margaret on the Altar of the Margaretenkapelle at Muggensturn (O. Schmitt, *Oberrheinische Plastik im ausgehenden Mittelalter*, Freiburg im Breisgau, 1924, pl. 94a). For her attitude and drapery, compare the type of Schongauer's engraving (Bartsch no. 27) and its development in Hans Baldung's drawings (for instance, no. 77, in C. Koch, *Die Zeichnungen Hans Baldung Griens*, Berlin, 1941). There are circumstantial and stylistic reasons for thinking the carver was Friedrich Hagenauer, who had been trained as a sculptor in Strasbourg and was in Augsburg from 1527 to 1532. He was the object of repeated complaint from the Augsburg sculptors' guild, who stated he abused his position as a medallist (*Konterfetter*), a craft exempt from guild control, to take work from sculptors: the complaints and his evasive reply are published by G. Habich ('Studien zur deutschen Renaissancemedaille' in *Jahrbuch der Königlich preussischen Kunstsammlungen*, vol. xxviii, 1907, pp. 269–72).

No full-length figures by Hagenauer are known, so comparison of style is limited to details in his models for medals: for example, Johann Kleinmüller, 1527, Bayerisches Nationalmuseum, Munich. (G. Habich, *Die deutschen Schaumünzen des 16. Jahrunderts*, Munich, 1929–34, vol. i, pt. i, p. 74, no. 484), for a similar adaptation to limestone of boxwood cutting formulas for fur and hair; Ursula Liegsalz, 1527, Munich (*op. cit.*, p. 76, no. 466) for the patterning of creases on the sleeves; and, for the carving of the Child's head, an undated model for a medal of an unknown young girl (*op. cit.*, p. 76, no. 487).

T. Müller, 'Frühe Beispiele der Retrospektive in der deutschen Plastik' in *Bayerische Akademie der Wissenschaften, Philosophisch-Historische Klasse, Sitzungsberichte*, vol. i, Munich, 1961, p. 20; and *Deutsche Plastik der Renaissance*, Königstein im Taunus, 1963, p. 27.

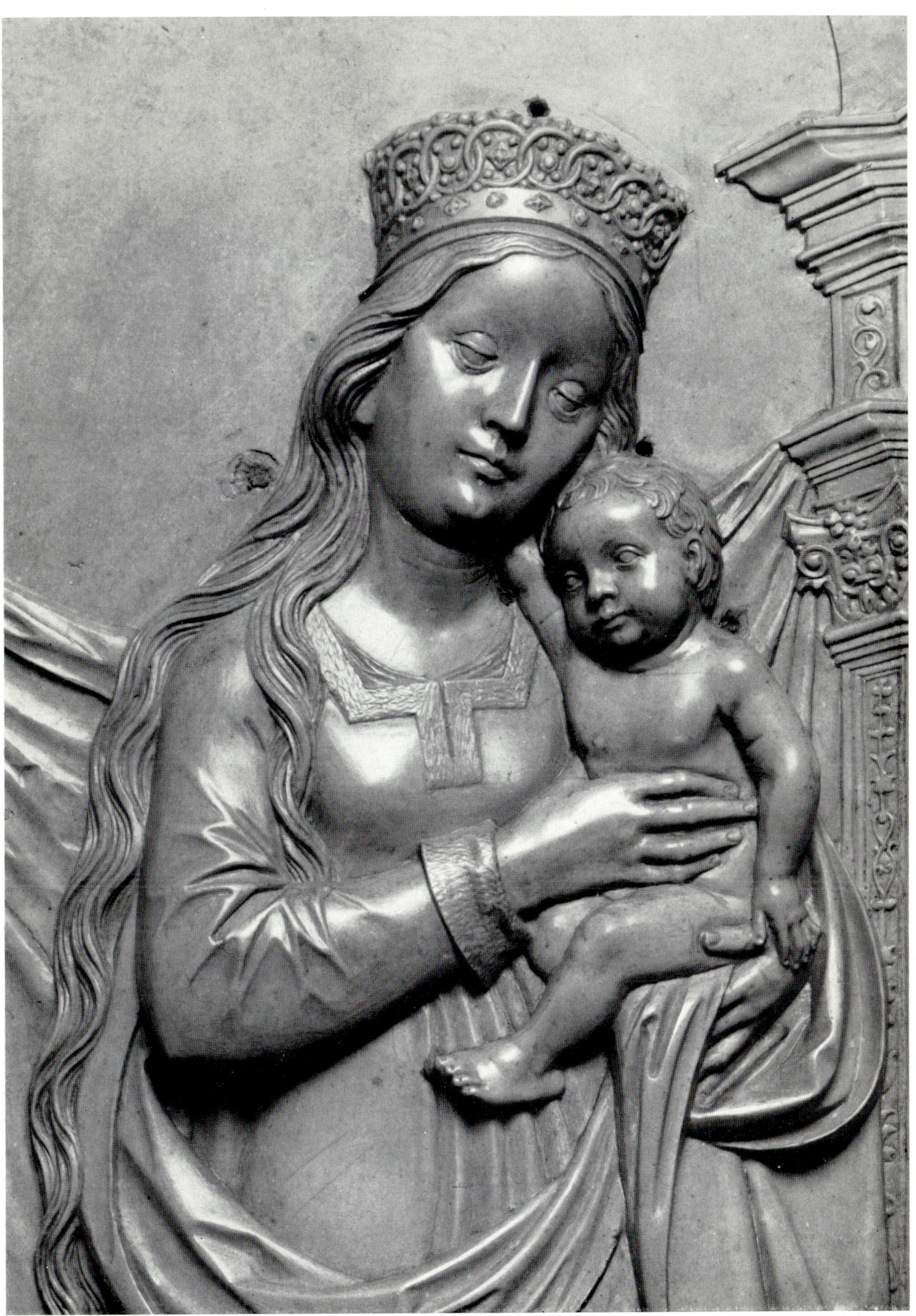

No. 20 THE JUDGMENT OF PARIS

Bavarian (Passau or Regensburg?). About 1530

Pearwood. H. 9¼ in. (23·5 cm.); w. 7 in. (18 cm.).
Museum no. 4528-1858

The relief is carved on three sections of wood joined vertically. The whole is now slightly concave, presumably by warping. A crack runs down from the top through the body of the horse. Fingers of the right hand of the foreground figure, Juno, are missing. The initials AD on the slab in the right foreground are in the form of Dürer's monogram and are probably a later addition.

Bought, 1858 (Philip Howard of Corby Castle).

Details in this relief are related to engravings by Cranach of 1508 and Altdorfer of 1511 (A. Bartsch, *Le peintre-graveur*, Leipzig, 1808, vol. vii, p. 291, no. 114, & vol. viii, p. 62, no. 60 respectively) but the composition seems independent. The carving is one of a class related in design to painting of the Danube school and showing a taste for forest landscapes; they have been associated with the Master I P, by whom there are signed works: for I P see, particularly, H. Seiberl in *Jahrbuch der Kunsthistorischen Sammlungen in Wien*, vol. xii, 1938, pp. 157–73, and A. Legner in the catalogue of the exhibition *Die Kunst der Donauschule 1490–1540*, Stift St Florian and Schlossmuseum Linz, 1965, pp. 278–91. The number of known carvings in this class has increased so much recently that a school or a very large workshop seems involved, rather than one master: it belongs in the period 1520–40 and probably in the area Passau–Salzburg–Regensburg. Individual identities within it are not clear, but the style of the London relief is (a) quite distinct from the carvings signed IP and (b) closest to the unsigned relief of Adam and Eve in the Kunstgewerbemuseum in Vienna, in which Eve repeats the Juno of the *Judgment of Paris*. The monogram AD might seem to relate the relief to two others in the Wallace Collection and the Palazzo Pitti in Florence with the signature Adam D, but the style is different and the monogram is here in the form of Dürer's. The IP style of relief was admired and copied during the Dürer revival around 1600 (T. Müller, 'Frühe Beispiele der Retrospektive in der deutschen Plastik' in *Bayerische Akademie der Wissenschaften, Philosophisch-Historische Klasse, Sitzungsberichte*, vol. i, 1961, pp. 22–5) and the monogram may have been added at that time.

M. Sauerlandt, *Kleinplastik der deutschen Renaissance*, Leipzig, 1927, p. 79; E. F. Bange, *Die Kleinplastik der deutschen Renaissance*, Munich, 1929, p. 50, pl. 45; H. Seiberl, 'Ein Salzburger Bildwerk im Prager Museum' in *Jahrbuch der Kunsthistorischen Sammlungen in Wien*, vol. xii, 1938, pp. 164–66; O. Kurz, 'A sculptor of the Danube School' in *Burlington Magazine*, vol. xci, 1949, pp. 217–18; A. Legner in Stift St Florian and Schlossmuseum Linz, *Die Kunst der Donauschule 1490–1540*, 1965, p. 290.

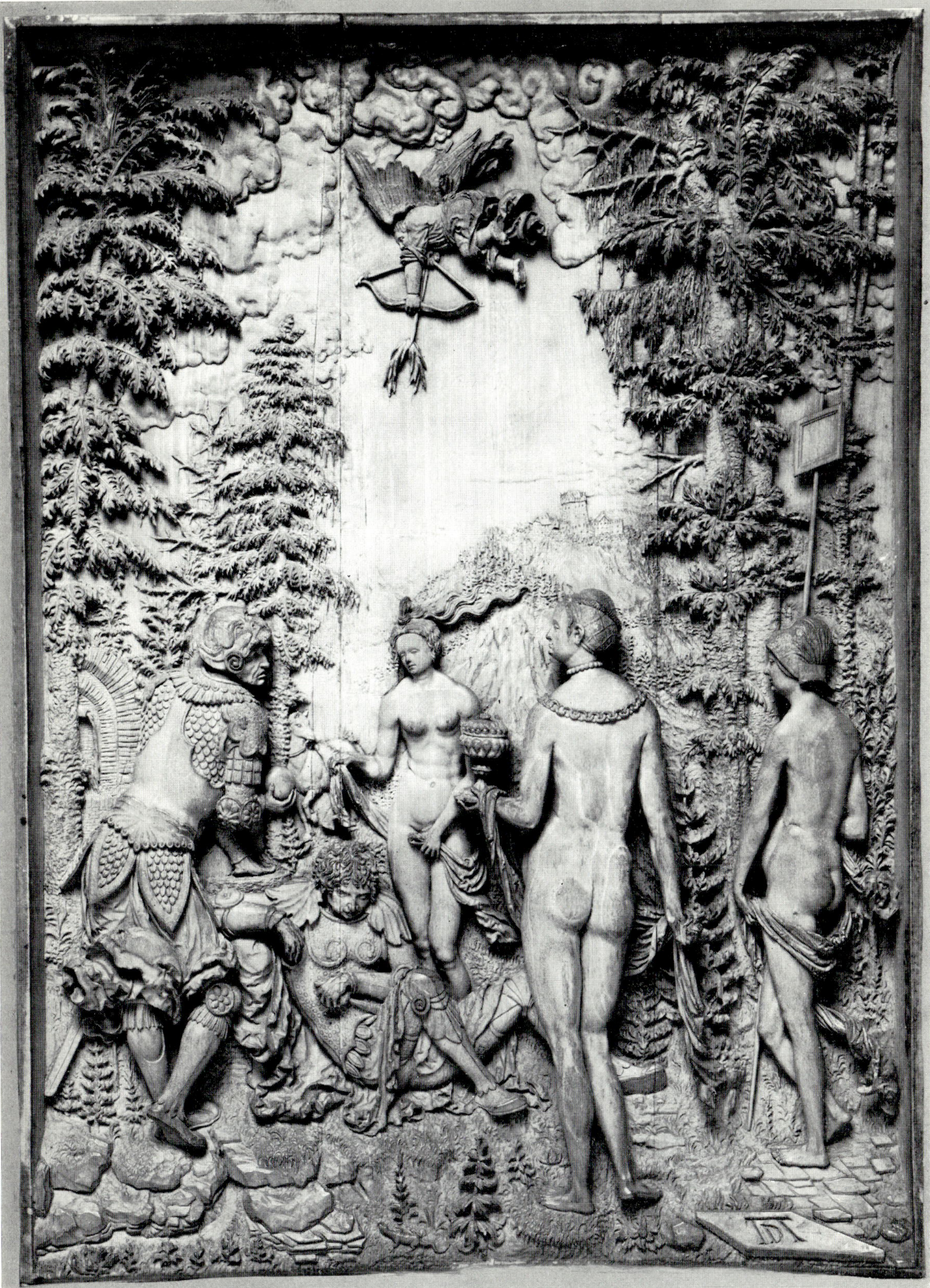